THE ARTIST'S
LIBRARY

The Artist's Library

A FIELD GUIDE

FROM THE LIBRARY AS INCUBATOR PROJECT

LAURA DAMON-MOORE
ERINN BATYKEFER

COFFEE HOUSE PRESS
MINNEAPOLIS
2014

COPYRIGHT © 2014 by Laura Damon-Moore and Erinn Batykefer
FOREWORD COPYRIGHT © 2014 by Jessica Pigza
COVER PHOTO "Pleated Language" © Lisa Occhipinti
COVER & BOOK DESIGN Linda S. Koutsky
Interior photos shot at the Minneapolis Central Library
LIBRARY AS INCUBATOR PROJECT LOGO designed by Rebecca Light

Coffee House Press books are available to the trade through our primary distributor, Consortium Book Sales & Distribution, cbsd.com or (800) 283-3572. For personal orders, catalogs, or other information, write to: info@coffeehousepress.org.

Coffee House Press is a nonprofit literary publishing house. Support from private foundations, corporate giving programs, government programs, and generous individuals helps make the publication of our books possible. We gratefully acknowledge their support in detail in the back of this book.

Visit us at at coffeehousepress.org.

LIBRARY OF CONGRESS CATALOGING-IN-PUBLICATION DATA

The artist's library : a field guide /
edited by Laura C. Damon-Moore and Erinn P. Batykefer.
    pages cm. — (Books in action)
    ISBN 978-1-56689-353-4
1. Libraries and community. 2. Libraries—Cultural programs.
3. Libraries—Social aspects. 4. Arts—Library resources.
5. Libraries—Problems, exercises, etc. 6. Creation (Literary, artistic, etc.)—Case studies. 7. Library users—Case studies.
    I. Damon-Moore, Laura C. II. Batykefer, Erinn.
Z716.4A78 2014
021.2—DC23
                                2013035168
                      PRINTED IN THE UNITED STATES
                      FIRST EDITION | FIRST PRINTING

ACKNOWLEDGMENTS

THIS LITTLE BOOK would not be possible without the help and support of many, many people. First and foremost, we need to express our heartfelt thanks to our team on the Library as Incubator Project: Katie Behrens, Holly Storck-Post, and Angela Terrab. You three make the work fun and inspired. A great deal of gratitude is due to Christina Jones (née Endres), our cofounder and a wonderful librarian; and to Dr. Louise Robbins, who was the Project's first advisor and continues to be a great cheerleader. Many thanks also to Trent Miller and Jesse Vieau, who not only supported the Project from the start, but also allow us to take over the Bubbler at Madison Public Library on a regular basis, and who have shaped our vision of the ideal arts-incubating library with their incredible work. The Library as Incubator Project would not be possible without the hundreds of artists, writers, performers, librarians, bloggers, and educators who work so hard to make the arts and art-making available to their communities, and who share their experiences and ideas with us. Jessica Pigza deserves a special shoutout for her lovely foreword and generally, for her support and enthusiasm. Thanks is also due to the fabulous staff of Coffee House Press, with special hat tips to Chris Fischbach, Caroline Casey, Anitra Budd, Linda Koutsky, and Kelsey Shanesey, all of whom have invested a great deal of time and energy to make this book project a reality.

DEDICATION

To JTB, who inspires my art-making.
—LDM

For my mom, who knew I was a librarian before I did.
—EB

Foreword

By Jessica Pigza, Rare Books Librarian,
New York Public Library

VISITING A LIBRARY HAS LONG BEEN A VERY HANDS-ON activity. You might run your hand along book spines as you browse, pull a volume off the shelf, and flip through pages in search of answers to your questions. Today, even though gathering information at the library is just as likely to include clicking and typing, the act of learning by doing—by tactile experience—retains its importance. And, in libraries both large and small, the power of hands-on creation today also manifests itself through makerspaces, collaborative skill-sharing partnerships, library scavenger hunts, and other creative arts programming for all ages.

What the founders of the Library as Incubator Project reveal so effectively and so enthusiastically is how the efforts of individual librarians and institutions to connect with their users in hands-on ways are part of a bigger picture. From its initial launch as an inspired student project, the Library as Incubator Project has quickly developed a much-deserved reputation for offering a one-stop shop—a place where a broad variety of creative lifelong learners, artists of all kinds, and librarians could

THE REGULARS COME IN QUIETLY,
SIT IN THE SAME PLACE EVERY DAY

gather to share ideas about programs that support hands-on creativity. I've been consistently impressed with their scope, surprised by their finds, and energized by their information. Along the way, I have learned how my own work to build a community engaged in handmade pursuits at my library fits into a much larger world of ideas and inspiration that is taking place in libraries all over the country.

In this book, Erinn and Laura extend their reach and offer an invaluable roadmap devoted to inviting more people to get creative with their libraries. An especially engaging feature of the book is its inclusive conception of who artists are. Dilettantes and professionals, performers and hobbyists, DIY devotees and tinkerers, crafters and poets, kids and grownups—all are welcome in *The Artist's Library*, just as they are welcome in libraries everywhere. In the pages of this book, this welcoming perspective is front and center as Erinn and Laura provide guidance and ideas for ways to use libraries as sources for collaboration, creation, and community connection. No matter what you are interested in making, this book will show how the library—its collections, its spaces, and its friendly staff—can join you on your creative journey.

—Jessica Pigza

Jessica Pigza is a librarian, an avid seamstress and knitter, and an enthusiast of books and other objects you can learn to make by hand. She oversees reader services and outreach as assistant curator of the Rare Book Division at the New York Public Library.

Introduction

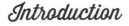

LIBRARIES HAVE HISTORICALLY BEEN PLACES WHERE PEOPLE come to educate themselves—to expand their recreational reading, to learn how to do everything from start a new business to bake the perfect cupcake. More and more, libraries not only provide information in the form of books (physical and digital), media, and periodicals, but also in the form of workshops, classes, and other opportunities for hands-on learning. Events on your library's calendar may cover topics like dance, filmmaking, grant writing, gardening, and resume writing.

> AN ARTIST IS A PERSON WHO LEARNS AND USES CREATIVE TOOLS AND TECHNIQUES TO MAKE NEW THINGS.

At the Library as Incubator Project, we believe the library is a place to connect and create. Through our website, social media networks, and national partnerships with libraries and arts organizations, we highlight the many ways libraries and artists can work together to incubate creativity.

So, how do we define *artist*? Librarians are an inclusive, egalitarian bunch, and libraries around the world support lifelong learning for the people in their communities, so we define *artist* more broadly than a museum might. To us, an artist is a person who learns and uses creative tools and techniques to make new things. An artist can be a professional musician, or a kid learning how to use sound-editing software in a library's digital lab. An artist can be a world-renowned author, or a senior citizen taking part in a memoir-writing workshop at her local library for the first time.

Creativity, like information, is free to everyone who steps into a library. Wherever you are in your artistic development—from finger painting during story time to researching themes for an interactive museum installation—the library can help to nurture and "incubate" your growth as a creative person. Which brings us to why we chose the term *incubator* to describe the lens through which we're viewing libraries and artists.

WE TELL O S WE ARE
STOR I S O NOT WAKE
TO   ITH A BLOW ON
     EAD WHAT ARE WE
E DING THEM FOR?

FRANZ KAFKA – LETTERS TO FRIENDS, FAMILY AND EDITORS – REFERENCE DEPARTMENT

Inspiration Incubators

The survey that got the Library as Incubator Project started several years ago posed this question to one hundred artists working in different media: "What does the phrase 'library as incubator' mean to you?"

We got everything from "nothing" to "it makes me think of chickens." Overwhelmingly, though, artists shared responses like these:

> An incubator is a warm place that encourages things to come to life. Information is the seed from which one grows. Information informs our work. Interaction with other users and librarians cross-pollinates our ideas and passions. Plus it takes time for development to occur, and presumably/hopefully a library is ongoing and reliable.

> I see a container where the artist dives in and gets inspiration. Pictures, scents, sounds, everything is packed in this incubator. It bubbles, it keeps percolating.

They're talking about inspiration, about creative development and growth, about ideas that can be fed by library collections, staff, and spaces. In the economic sector, the term *incubator* indicates something entrepreneurial in nature. Business incubators are places where small business owners can grow and develop professionally, surrounded by resources and support in a nurturing environment.

What is so exciting to us, and why we loved the idea of naming our project the Library as Incubator Project, is that libraries can and do offer the same kind of "incubating" support to artists at every step of the creative process—from inception, to making or production, to the promotion of a finished work.

There are a lot of people who use the library, consciously or unconsciously, as a creativity sandbox. Book artist Carol Chase Bjerke, one of our earliest interviewees, once found a little book of photography at her library while researching something else. The images and ideas it contained eventually helped her create a gorgeous pop-up book called *Point of Departure.* She didn't start the project immediately after finding the book, but the inherent serendipity of unexpectedly discovering a book that captured her imagination set the gears in motion. There are others who come to the library partway through the creative process, to expand upon or enhance a current project with library research: authors of historical fiction, poets looking to explore a visual resource, dramaturges digging into sources to get background for set or costume design.

> LIBRARIES CAN AND DO OFFER THE SAME KIND OF "INCUBATING" SUPPORT TO ARTISTS AT EVERY STEP OF THE CREATIVE PROCESS—FROM INCEPTION, TO MAKING OR PRODUCTION, TO THE PROMOTION OF A FINISHED WORK.

Libraries can offer a place for artists to actually work, too—in studio or making spaces, at tables with laptop plugs, in quiet study rooms, and in café areas. These spaces provide a change of scenery, a place to wander and break free of creative blocks, or to experiment "outside of your art" through workshops, artist demonstrations, or gallery shows, all of which can shake up the creative brain and offer a fresh perspective.

In a growing trend, people publish and produce written works through libraries. When they do, the library can serve as a promotional space for the finished works (just as they do for blockbuster novels) through collections, displays, and book recommendation services. Authors hold readings to promote their new work in libraries. Theater artists and musicians perform. Visual artists show their work in gallery spaces. Libraries also provide resources that artists can use to promote their work outside of the library, including how-to books, publishing industry guides, marketing resources, accounting textbooks, online marketplace guides, and so much more.

Come One, Come All

One of the things we focus on at the Library as Incubator Project is arts-related library programs. We see arts programming as a way to attract new and perhaps different users to libraries; to expose a wide range of people to arts of all kinds; to promote local arts organizations and individual artists; and to provide opportunities for library users to interact with artists in their community, which allows them to learn from peers and develop their own artistic skills.

The goal isn't to say that libraries should compete with community centers, museums, or art centers, but rather, we encourage libraries to become active partners with such institutions to ensure that the needs and expectations of their communities are met and exceeded. In line with "Creative Placemaking," a paper published by the National Endowment for the Arts in 2012, we consider libraries to be excellent examples of "creative crucibles"—one of many satellite art-making spaces that contribute to the cultural and economic well-being of a community.

A key reason for our work to promote libraries as creative spaces is that, with few exceptions, library users have equal access to the space, collections, and people in libraries. In this democratic space, professional artists and writers can work alongside those testing out a new artistic skill for the first time, or "creative hobbyists" who simply enjoy the process of art-making. We champion the idea that the open and unpretentious library can offer a return to the quiet, unselfconscience art-making that so many adults "grow out of" after childhood.

How to Use This Book

In this volume, we share some of the inspiring artist stories we've collected to suggest new ways you can use your library to increase productivity, inspire new work, and support a creative life.

In Chapter 1: Exploring the Library as Subject and Chapter 2: Finding Inspiration in Library Collections, we share some big-picture concepts—inspiration found in the library as an architectural space, as a philosophical idea, and as a nearly endless collection of books, music, magazines, and digital materials. Chapter 3: Using the Library for Creative Research dives into examples of world-class artists who explore complex historical and political subjects in their work, and suggests creative techniques for researching subjects and expressing new ideas in your chosen medium. In Chapters 4 and 5, Using the Library as a Space to Work and Using the Library as an Arts Venue, we take a closer look at how the library can serve as a workspace for a variety of artists, and how its place at the center of the community, available to all people, makes it an ideal venue for showcasing work in library display galleries and for performing new music and theater productions. We share important perspectives in Chapter 6: Creating Successful Programming Partnerships with Libraries, to help you collaborate with librarians in your area to create exciting programs that can serve both artists and community members. Chapter 7: Using the Library to Build Your Arts Organization or Business, offers practical tips on using the library to get your art-related business up and running.

At the end of each chapter, we include hands-on, artist-inspired exercises that you can incorporate into your creative brainstorming practices. Some of them are tips and suggestions for ways to get to know your library and the resources it has to offer. Others are designed to kick-start your creative brain and get you making something. In the back of the book, you'll find a custom bibliography of digital collections and library-curated websites that offer inspiring source material you can access from anywhere, for free.

Our intent is for you to wear out this book: draw in the margins, make notes, paste in pictures and Post-its, and use it to fill up your own notebooks. Our goal—like any good arts-incubating librarian—is to inform and inspire you as you discover your library, or discover new ways to use it. We hope you'll use this book to create something new, and that you'll share your story with us when you do.

—Erinn Batykefer and Laura Damon-Moore

Cofounders and Managing Editors
The Library as Incubator Project
Madison, Wisconsin, February 2013

Authors' Note

LIBRARIES

Before we get started, we'd like to give a brief overview of the types of libraries that are out there in the world—we discuss some, but not all, in this book.

PUBLIC LIBRARIES

Public libraries are usually part of a city or town government structure, funded by tax dollars and private donations, and free and open to the public. They may be connected to a community center, a city hall, or they may stand alone. Public library collections are made up of general-interest items, such as popular fiction and nonfiction books, movies, music, video and computer games, and so on. Public library programs may include computer workshops, early literacy programs like story times, summer reading programs, book clubs, and lectures and workshops on everything from gardening to beer brewing.

ACADEMIC LIBRARIES

Academic libraries are found on university or college campuses. Their services and collections are geared toward students, faculty, and visiting scholars of the institution. Some academic libraries may offer limited borrowing privileges and services for members of the general public. Many academic libraries host online digital collections of items that have been digitized in an effort to preserve material and make it available for study by a wide range of people. Collections in academic libraries support in-depth scholarship and research on a variety of topics (individual libraries will usually have strengths in particular disciplines, such as artist books, Middle Eastern studies, or theater for youth). Academic library staff offer instruction on how to conduct library research, how to cite references properly, and how to organize your research materials effectively, as well as provide traditional reference assistance for people working on research projects. Academic libraries often host exhibitions of their materials and of student and faculty research and work.

ARCHIVES

Archives are collections of primary sources and artifacts (letters, business reports, postcards, scrapbooks, photographs, and so forth) that collectively document the history of an individual, a business, a school, a town, or a building. Unlike libraries, which have "managed" collections (items are constantly added in and weeded out), the purpose of an archive is to represent a moment in history as fully as possible. Archives are usually part of a larger institution like a college or university, a historical society, or a public library. Finding and using the items in an archive often requires some advance work—you'll need to obtain a finding aid (a document that tells you what's in an archival collection and how the archive is organized), and you may need to set up an appointment ahead of time.

SPECIAL COLLECTIONS

Special collections are frequently part of large research institutions like a university, a museum, or a major research library. They tend to focus on a small number of disciplines, such as ornithology or the history of medicine, and may house rare books or a complete collection of materials related to a specific subject. A major goal for special collections staff is to preserve these materials for posterity, meaning that not all items will be accessible to the general public. An advance appointment and prior knowledge of the collection and what you're looking for is nearly always required when dealing with special collections; some institutions may also require a letter of reference.

SPECIAL LIBRARIES

There are a number of libraries that fall under the heading of "special libraries." More often than not, whether a library is categorized as "special" depends on whether it fits into the broad categories of public, academic, or school libraries. Special libraries might have an unusual focus (such as a wine library) or a very specialized collection and staff, like medical libraries, law libraries, and corporate libraries. Special libraries vary in terms of public access to their collections; some (corporate libraries, for example) may be completely private, while others may offer limited access. You'll want to check well in advance to see if the library you want to use is available for public use, and you'll probably need to make an appointment prior to your visit.

SCHOOL LIBRARIES

School libraries provide resources and services to support the curriculum of κ–12 educational institutions. School librarians or library media specialists are teachers who instruct in media, digital literacy, and research practices.

THE ARTISTS

The artists in this book were all initially interviewed for the Library as Incubator Project website. They come from a range of geographic locations and artistic backgrounds, work in a variety of mediums, and use libraries in a multitude of ways. One thing they have in common is that libraries and literature are integral to their work, and they champion the library as a vital part of a thriving creative existence.

The Supplies

If you're a writer, artist, doodler, scribbler, crafter . . . really, a "maker" of any sort, you probably already have an arsenal of favorite and trusted supplies. In case you're curious, though, we pulled together a list of our most-used art supplies, to give you an idea of what we're using when we do the exercises in this book.

☐ Composition notebook	☐ Book pages
☐ Box of Crayola crayons	☐ Regular pencil
☐ Box of colored pencils	☐ Rotary cutter
☐ Flair pen	☐ Self-healing mat
☐ Watercolor paints	☐ Fabric fat quarters
☐ Library card catalog cards	☐ Decoupage materials
☐ School glue	☐ Origami papers
☐ Dictionary	☐ Charcoal
☐ Post-its	☐ Pastels
☐ X-Acto knife	☐ Chalks
☐ Scissors	☐ Index cards

CHAPTER 1

Exploring the Library as Subject

I F YOU'VE EVER EXPERIENCED A CREATIVE BLOCK, you've probably wished there was a way to just remove yourself from the pressure of not writing or drawing or making, some place you could go to empty your brain of all the "should" and simply wander around, discovering evocative stories, beautiful images, inspiring music—anything that might accidentally-on-purpose jump-start your creative brain. You might've also wished there were a tour guide for such a place, someone who could help steer you through all the endless stuff that might inspire you and take you straight to the stuff that works (with a few interesting detours along the way to introduce things you didn't know about).

This place exists, and no matter where you live, it's probably not far away: it's called the library.

In this chapter, we examine the inherently inspiring nature of libraries—from the monumental architecture used to build them, to the basic concept of free access to information for all, to new and creative riffs on discovery and inspiration found in familiar stacks and online catalogs.

Capturing the Unexpected

THE LIBRARY ITSELF CAN BE AN EVOCATIVE SUBJECT. THE world over, architects have designed libraries to communicate the incredible power of knowledge. Trolling the web for "beautiful libraries" yields a treasure trove of stunning images: gilded domes, columns, and friezes that hearken back to classical Greek architecture; marble floors; and mahogany shelves—and that's just from older specimens!

In this section, we take a look at how libraries, both grand and practical, are part of a longstanding story of human knowledge and experience. Our example here is a photographer who deliberately uses vintage film, cameras, and developing processes to document libraries. Jamie Powell Sheppard's *The*

"

THE WORLD OVER, ARCHITECTS HAVE DESIGNED LIBRARIES TO COMMUNICATE THE INCREDIBLE POWER OF KNOWLEDGE.

"

Libraries Project seeks to capture the unexpected, to force viewers to appreciate libraries not only as architectural marvels, but also as an often-overlooked force for good that should be supported and preserved. Her work goes beyond simple composition, light, and shadow to comment on the larger social narrative of libraries and the people who use them.

JAMIE POWELL SHEPPARD

Jamie Powell Sheppard is drawn to what others might not notice—a trait that's useful in her work as a photographer, and especially poignant considering her subject matter. Her ongoing photo-documentary work, *The Libraries Project*, began when she was working at a library in Tennessee. "After several years of photographer's block," she says, "I started photographing my own library, as well as others in our consortium. A few years later I was living in Louisville, Kentucky, where I encountered my first Carnegie library. I was smitten and my inspiration was fully reawakened."

Jamie's project engages with the stunning narrative of Andrew Carnegie, who famously built 1,689 "Carnegie libraries" between 1883 and 1929 in the United States. No one who applied for a Carnegie grant and agreed to his terms was turned down, which means that libraries were built in many small towns and rural outposts that probably wouldn't have had any cultural anchors otherwise. Today, they are disappearing; they are old buildings, usually too small for significant collections even in the smallest of towns, and often costly and difficult to rewire and refurbish.

"Part of my desire is to document these graceful buildings before we lose them forever," Jamie says, "but I also want people to rediscover their libraries, to realize that they offer so much more than just free babysitting, and to celebrate that. I believe that if I could show people their libraries from a different perspective, they'd develop pride and be less willing to lose such a gift. If nothing else, I'd like them to say 'Wait, that's from *my* library? I've gotta go back now and look!'"

➤ EXERCISES

☐ Take a moment to really look at your library. Where is it? How does the location and design make you feel about what's inside the walls? How might you communicate similar ideas and themes in your own work?

☐ Check out some online galleries of beautiful libraries around the world (our favorites are listed in the Resources section on page 199). Pick your favorite and sketch a scene that might take place there.

☐ Find a hidden corner in your home library. Take a few moments to describe what you can see, hear, smell, and feel from where you are sitting. Which titles can you see in the stacks? What is the light like? What sorts of noises and activity can you perceive? The library is alive, and you are listening to its heartbeat. Record your ideas in a notebook.

Playing with the Notion of the "Library"

WHAT IS A LIBRARY, IF NOT THE REPRESENTATION OF AN idea? People the world over have long believed that information and knowledge are so important to preserve—and more recently, make available to the public—that special civic and educational structures should be dedicated to the practice. The contents of a library make up a working document of what a community values as much as a particular book, song, or painting is a document of a subject.

Our artist example for this idea is Doreen Kennedy, who decided to zoom in on one library's collection for a recent photographic project. Her work focuses on the small details recorded in library books—date stamps, dog-eared pages, broken spines—that come together to create a map of people's interest and curiosity, and their interactions with knowledge and information.

DOREEN KENNEDY

Doreen Kennedy introduces her series, *Portrait of a Library,* with a glimpse into her childhood fascination with books as artifacts: "I have been visiting local libraries since childhood," she says. "I am fascinated by the idea that you can borrow books for free and that these books will pass through many hands before reaching you. Each book has its personal history documented by the date stamps in the inside cover, a new reader with every new date.

"Looking at the dates, I would wonder about the other people who had read the book. Did they finish it? Perhaps they just read a few pages and lost interest? Sometimes a clue about previous readers would be left in the form of a bookmark, a receipt from a supermarket, a postcard from a sunny location, or a scrap of paper torn from a notebook. [Recently discovered] routing slips suggested books ordered from other library branches and made me consider the motivations of the people who sought these specific titles."

> " I AM FASCINATED BY THE IDEA THAT YOU CAN BORROW BOOKS FOR FREE AND THAT THESE BOOKS WILL PASS THROUGH MANY HANDS BEFORE REACHING YOU. "

Doreen's lifelong interest in the many human stories that library books record—in addition to their printed stories—peaked in 2010, when she approached the public library in the Dublin suburb of Dalkey about using the library as the subject of a photographic project. "My idea was to visit the library a number of times to document its contents. My visits began in August when I started the work of photographing the books and other aspects of the library space. Across several visits I made over a thousand photographs.

"The resulting images became a series of photomontage grids, diptychs, and single-image photographs of book details and the library interior [that] documents the contents of a library. Its history of borrowing is marked by the beautiful worn book covers, broken spines, creased pages, and intriguing date stamps."

☐ Pick out a book from a shelf in your library. It could be one you've read and know well, or one you've never seen before but like the look of. Look at its table of contents. Read the introduction and maybe a page or two from the first chapter to familiarize yourself with its subject matter. Speculate for a moment on where this book has been before you held it in your hands. Who might have checked it out over the course of its life in this library? Draw your idea of the book's journey in a notebook.

☐ Wander through a genre section of your library (e.g., romance, westerns, science fiction, mystery). Let the condition of the books tell a story about the books in this section. What do the spine, corners, and repairs tell you about the pages inside a book? See what totally inconclusive, non-scientific conclusions you can draw about this section based strictly on what you can see as you walk along. Jot down your ideas. Later, see if you can write a few paragraphs about that section in the style of a travel guide, pointing out "landmarks" and "undiscovered treasures."

Examining the Living, Breathing Library

IF YOU KNOW WHERE TO LOOK, THE LIBRARY CAN BE FULL OF unexpected surprises. Despite lingering stereotypes that cast libraries as rigidly silent spaces and librarians as severe, bun-headed women, libraries have always been about juxtapositions and discovery. Have you ever gone to the library stacks in search of a particular book, only to emerge bearing three or four (or ten!) other titles you found shelved in the same area? This happy accident is no accident at all: librarians study the importance of serendipity in the act of what we call "title discovery," and the best library designs aim to increase it.

Great art works the same way, fueled by accidental juxtapositions that suggest new interpretations, new ideas, and even book recommendations. Chris Gaul, a visual artist and designer who recently completed an artist residency in a library, riffs on the concept of title discovery in order to reimagine the library as an intuitive space that fosters curiosity and investigation in a variety of delightfully unexpected ways.

> **LIBRARIES HAVE ALWAYS BEEN ABOUT JUXTAPOSITIONS AND DISCOVERY.**

Chris Gaul

Chris Gaul is fascinated by simple, everyday objects. "When things like bus tickets or library cards are well designed, they can create moments of playfulness and discovery in daily life," he says. His time spent in the University of Technology–Sydney (Australia) library as artist-in-residence generated a lot of ideas in this vein.

Chris's projects range from the simple to the wildly complex, but all hinge on the idea of how we find and value objects—often books. Here are a few concepts he worked on while at the UTS library:

"Book Babble . . . lets listeners wear a pair of headphones and wander the library listening to books reading themselves aloud. The headphones are connected to an RFID [radio-frequency identification] reader and a mobile device. The RFID reader senses nearby books, and the mobile app finds the content of those books and reads them into the headphones. As the listener wanders through different parts of the library, the tone of the babble drifts through different subjects

"Library Tuner [repurposes] a vintage hi-fi tuner so that listeners can turn the dial to tune in to the different Dewey 'frequencies' for books in the library.

"Another project involves repurposing a vintage rotary telephone so that listeners can use the call numbers of books to call the books on the telephone."

Not all of Chris's ideas are so technically complex. This one changes how patrons find new books, and how librarians collect data about how their collections are used, simply by relabeling the library's bookdrop chutes:

> Currently borrowers return books through one of three chutes based on the call number of the book. Replacing these Dewey number labels with new labels (for example, "I loved this book," or even "I didn't like this book," or "I didn't read this book") not only gives the borrower a moment to reflect on their reading experience but also provides the library with valuable data. For example, it would be straightforward to create a shelf of recent returns that the last reader loved.

Even if your library isn't home to an artist residency, creative interpretations of the library abound. There are infinite and unexpected ways to understand a library and its collections, and to incubate a wandering curiosity that can fuel creative expression.

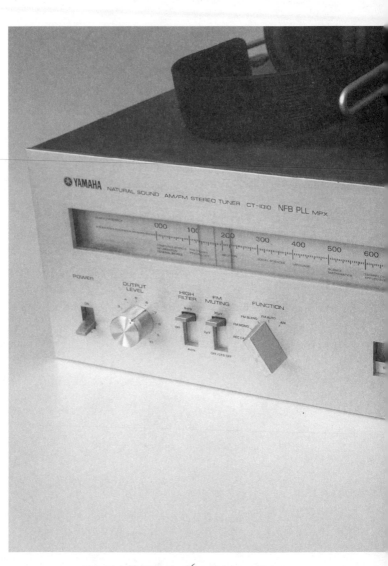

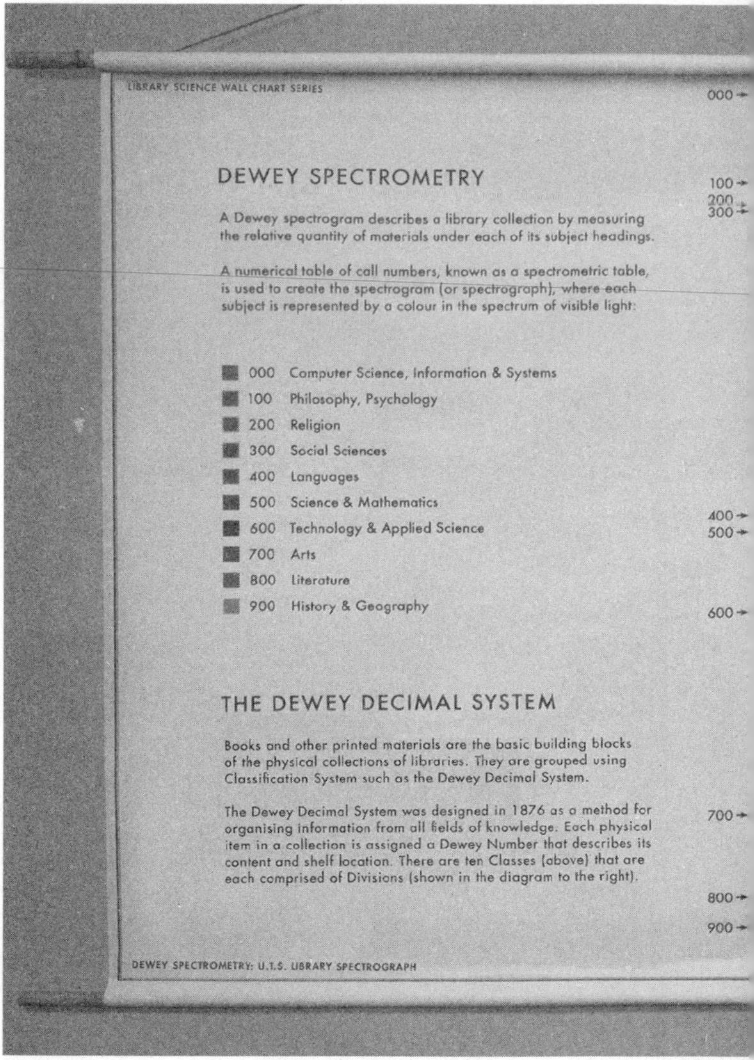

000 →

DEWEY SPECTROMETRY

100 →
200 →
300 →

A Dewey spectrogram describes a library collection by measuring the relative quantity of materials under each of its subject headings.

A numerical table of call numbers, known as a spectrometric table, is used to create the spectrogram (or spectrograph), where each subject is represented by a colour in the spectrum of visible light:

- 000 Computer Science, Information & Systems
- 100 Philosophy, Psychology
- 200 Religion
- 300 Social Sciences
- 400 Languages
- 500 Science & Mathematics
- 600 Technology & Applied Science
- 700 Arts
- 800 Literature
- 900 History & Geography

400 →
500 →

600 →

THE DEWEY DECIMAL SYSTEM

Books and other printed materials are the basic building blocks of the physical collections of libraries. They are grouped using Classification System such as the Dewey Decimal System.

The Dewey Decimal System was designed in 1876 as a method for organising information from all fields of knowledge. Each physical item in a collection is assigned a Dewey Number that describes its content and shelf location. There are ten Classes (above) that are each comprised of Divisions (shown in the diagram to the right).

700 →

800 →

900 →

DEWEY SPECTROMETRY: U.1.S. LIBRARY SPECTROGRAPH

U.T.S. LIBRARY SPECTROGRAM

The spectrogram to the left is comprised of the 813,647 items with Dewey Numbers in the Library of the University of Technology, Sydney.

COMPARING LIBRARIES

Spectrographic Surveys are useful tools for comparing the structure of library collections. The diagrams below show the spectral variations between four libraries:

University of Technology, Sydney Library

University of Wollongong Library

Australian Catholic University Library

University of Western Sydney, Library

Relative sizes of collections:

DATA COURTESY OF THE LIBRARIES LISTED ABOVE AND CURRENT JULY 2013.

◄ EXERCISES

☐ Play with everyday objects in your library: Grab a stack of books, a golf pencil or two (find them next to the computer catalog), a magazine, and other easily moveable items. Hole up in a study room or at a worktable and arrange your objects in front of you. What are their relationships to one another? If these objects were alive, what would they worry about? Be excited about? What secrets would they hold? What do their nights look like? How do they interact with each other when the library is closed?

☐ Think about how you go about finding information, whether it is a new novel to read, a field guide for local birds, or a medical study. Make a list of all the different ways you find information. Do you do research on your own? Ask friends for recommendations? Ask a librarian? Use an app on your phone or computer? How would you reorganize your home library to facilitate your style of title discovery? Jot down your ideas for ways to reorganize your own collections of information.

☐ Are you interested in what other library users thought of a particular book? Talk with your librarian about implementing a patron recommendation display or shelf at the library.

Libraries and You

No matter where you go, there is likely to be a library. This can be a wonderful, grounding element in a creative life—a life often spent moving around, either from place to place or from idea to idea. No matter how far you travel, a library will likely be a part of your community, and no matter how quickly you leap between ideas as you pursue the next great project, that library can help you find the information you need to create something extraordinary—even if it means ordering rare or out-of-print books from somewhere else.

> **LIBRARIES REPRESENT AN EXCITING SENSE OF POSSIBILITY, AS WELL AS A SENSE OF COMFORT.**

Joseph Mills, a poet who has moved quite a lot, gets a new library card each time as a way to anchor himself in a new town. To him, libraries represent an exciting sense of possibility, as well as a sense of comfort—and we think this is the perfect place from which to make consistently thoughtful and meaningful art.

Joseph Mills

"Lending libraries are beautiful in their basic ideals. In enabling people to educate themselves, they are the most empowering and humanistic of institutions."

So says Joseph Mills, a poet whose creative curiosity has been nurtured by dozens of libraries throughout his life. "Forty years after getting my own first card (at the Shawnee Public Library in Fort Wayne, Indiana), I still feel a sense of amazement at having access to so many materials," he says. "In a very real way, libraries have shaped who I am."

It's interesting to think about artists' identities in this way. What does one need to be creative and to make art? What environmental factors do you need to be an artist? For Joseph, many of the elements he needed to write came together at the library:

- A space that was part of the community, but that also respected individual privacy

- Freely available collections of interesting materials and the freedom to explore and discover new things

- Capable people who could help find tricky materials and suggest other things he might find interesting

Throw in good lighting, comfortable seating, and long hours, and this is a recipe for many artists' ideal library. But it is also a place that is conducive to creativity, a place to invent and nurture new projects. "When I walk into my library," Joseph says, "it feels like optimism and hope. It simultaneously offers a sense of adventure and safety."

If Librarians Were Honest

J. Mills

a book indeed sometimes debauched me from my work
—BENJAMIN FRANKLIN

If librarians were honest,
they wouldn't smile, or act
welcoming. They would say,
*You need to be careful. Here
be monsters.* They would say,
*These rooms house heathens
and heretics, murderers and
maniacs, the deluded, desperate,
and dissolute.* They would say,
*These books contain knowledge
of death, desire, and decay,
betrayal, blood, and more blood;
each is a Pandora's box, so why
would you want to open one?*
They would post danger
signs warning that contact
might result in mood swings,
severe changes in vision,
and mind-altering effects.
If librarians were honest
they would admit the stacks
can be more seductive and
shocking than porn. After all,
once you've seen a few
breasts, vaginas, and penises,

more is simply more,
a comforting banality,
but the shelves of a library
contain sensational novelties,
a scandalous, permissive mingling
of Malcolm X, Marx, Melville,
Merwin, Millay, Milton, Morrison,
and anyone can check them out,
taking them home or to some corner
where they can be debauched
and impregnated with ideas.
If librarians were honest,
they would say, *No one
spends time here without being
changed. Maybe you should
go home. While you still can.*

☐ Book a tour of your local library with a librarian as tour guide. (If you're a recent transplant, this will be a great excuse to learn about the wealth of collections and services available to you as a resident or student, but even if you've lived in the same town for years, this can be an illuminating exercise.) Bring a short list of materials and subjects that are evocative for you and facilitate your creative process, and ask your tour guide to give you an overview of the whole library with particular emphasis on the topics that interest you (Foreign films? Local history? Image databases? Cookbooks? Tai chi classes?). Take notes.

☐ Think back to the first library you ever visited. Write about or draw moments from that experience. What was exciting, frustrating, comforting, or playful about the experience? What was the first item you remember checking out of a library? Did you think of the fact that you were sharing that item with many other people? Why or why not?

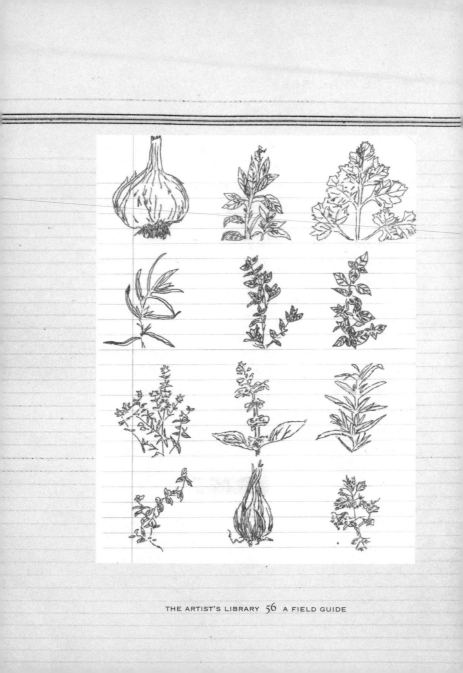

CHAPTER 2

Finding Inspiration in Library Collections

IN CHAPTER I WE EXPLORED THE LIBRARY AS SPACE, and even as something of a living organism. Now it's time to dig into the contents of the library—the books, the newspapers and magazines, the videos and audiobooks, the digitized images and documents. Artists, writers, and performers regularly find all sorts of inspiration for their creative projects in the library. Some zero in on a particular book, while others discover intriguing finds when browsing a specific shelf, stack, or section.

On the Shelf

WHEN IT COMES TO FINDING CREATIVE INSPIRATION, the beauty of libraries is that they offer multiple access points—ways to dig into the "stuff" they contain. (Remember that thing called title discovery? That's what we're talking about.) You can explode this out to the point of talking about an entire building or entire collection of materials, or you can narrow it down to a single chapter in a single book. Or you can fall somewhere in the middle—a particular section, a particular shelf.

In this section, we explore a library bookshelf, or bookstack. It's at this level of exploration that many happy accidents occur: combing the shelves for a certain title or author, you stumble upon a volume that in turn inspires a new creative direction.

Such was the case for book artist Carol Chase Bjerke. A chance meeting between Carol and a small, unassuming volume led to a moment of creative clarity that sparked an entirely new artistic adventure.

Carol Chase Bjerke

For Carol Chase Bjerke, the question "have libraries informed or inspired your artistic work?" brings to mind a moment of serendipity. As a graduate student working on a research paper, she was browsing the stacks at her university library. Carol was running her fingers along the spines of books when an untitled volume caught her eye.

"I pulled it off the shelf to learn that it was an odd little photography book called *Posing for the Camera: Tips for the Photographer and Tips for the Model*. There were no photographs in it, but the diagrams intrigued me. I wanted to spend more time with it, so I checked it out along with other materials, even though it had nothing to do with my needs at the time."

The book sat on her crowded desk for the rest of the term. She picked it up only to return it to the library at the end of the semester after a trip she had planned was canceled.

> FLIPPING THROUGH THE PAGES OF THIS BOOK, I EXPERIENCED ONE OF THOSE EUREKA MOMENTS WHEN A WHOLE NEW CREATIVE PROJECT IS BORN.

"Flipping through the pages of this book," writes Carol, "I experienced one of those eureka moments when a whole new creative project is born. Page after page of the diagrams and text inspired ideas for a pop-up book that would be an imaginary journey to all the places I would have spent the summer had the actual trip occurred. I renewed the book, arranged for an independent study project, and set about to make my *Point of Departure* pop-up book that has since traveled to numerous locations and exhibitions, and inspired several other projects and reviews."

For Carol, the stacks of her library inspired an entirely new creative project—though the inspiration didn't come immediately. Developing a creative project takes time. "Presumably, hopefully," Carol writes, "a library is ongoing and reliable."

▢ Choose an object or symbol that has meaning for you. Research its sociological, cultural, archetypal, and/or historical connections. Invent an appropriate book fold or structure to present some aspect of its meaning.*

▢ Check out several reference books unrelated to your current project. Some ideas include dream dictionaries, bestiaries, illustrated botanical or animal field guides, tarot dictionaries, collections of song lyrics, and fakebooks. Spread four to five out on a table or floor and page through them slowly, comparing the pages. What connections, if any, do you see between the books you picked? Are there any unexpected links to your current project? Write down your ideas in a notebook, or draw a map that depicts the connections you've discovered.

☐ Visit a section of your local library that you don't usually frequent. Maybe it's the poetry shelf, the picture books, the photography shelf, or the local history room. Spend some time looking at the titles on the shelves. Pull books off the shelves and flip through them, either in the library or at home. What do you notice? Wait one day. What do you remember reading or seeing in these books? Jot down a few notes (e.g., "a dog," "yellow house," and so on). What images or ideas stick in your mind?

*Contributed by Christi Weindorf.

On the Page

FOR MANY OF US, READING AND MAKING ART ARE CLOSELY connected, especially when we're very young. As children, favorite books are often ones that inspire the urge to make something: a drawing, a poem, a play scene. For one of our writers, books like Pamela Stearns's *Into the Painted Bear Lair*, Madeleine L'Engle's *A Wrinkle in Time*, and E. L. Konigsburg's *From the Mixed-Up Files of Mrs. Basil E. Frankweiler* compelled her to grab her basket of Magic Markers and draw scenes, objects, and characters—eventually expanding into her own odd worlds and parallel universes. Art-making extends the act of reading, solidifying ideas and concepts we've picked up from the text.

In this section, we look at two examples of artists who explore texts by putting pen to paper. Graphic designer and illustrator Stephen Crowe read James Joyce's tome *Finnegans Wake* before taking on the self-imposed project of illustrating the whole volume. The complicated text offers him a new, exciting challenge that combines literary analysis and art-making. Our next example, illustrator Dan Augustine, climbs into the world of fifty famous literary characters, depicting small moments from "their" worlds in his series *Everything is Fragile*.

STEPHEN CROWE

*W*ake *in Progress*, Stephen Crowe's web-based project, chronicles his goal of illustrating all of *Finnegans Wake*, by James Joyce. The result is weird and wonderful, providing an amazing visual path into a notoriously difficult text.

Stephen got the idea for the project from Zak Smith, an illustrator who took it upon himself to create an image for every page of Thomas Pynchon's *Gravity's Rainbow*. When Stephen found himself looking for a way to incorporate illustration into his spare time, Smith's project came to mind.

Stephen's decision to use *Finnegans Wake* as the foundation of an ongoing (and seriously long-term) illustration project was threefold.

Our cubehouse still rocks as earwitness to the thunder of his arafatas but we hear also through successive ages that shebby choruysh of unkalified muzzlenimiissilehims that would blackguardise the whitestone ever hurtleturtled out of heaven.

First, I wanted to choose a book that would really benefit from illumination—I didn't want to just draw people talking to each other in different rooms. Second, I'd long wanted to reread [*Finnegans Wake*] more carefully (I read it once before and understood as much as I could of it). Finally, it was a kind of cowardly hedge against self-doubt. I knew that there were many illustrators better than me, but I bet that very few of them had read *Finnegans Wake*. So it was like my own personal niche.

So how to choose what to draw from the many "moments" depicted in the text? Drawing what's actually happening on the page is difficult, because there is often more than one thing taking place at the same time. Instead, Stephen finds "visual metaphors" that suggest (rather than directly illustrate) each moment, which in turn makes it easier to "create an impression of thematic and narrative development."

"My general method is to read each chapter several times, worry over the hardest parts for what seems like years, and try to choose a sentence from each page that both suggests a visual metaphor and leads the narrative forward. Sometimes I just have to give up and draw a pretty picture. Sometimes I'll struggle for weeks to come up with a strong image, and sometimes it will come to me all of a sudden."

For Stephen, books, even "difficult" texts like *Finnegans Wake*, provide structure and that most basic of creative needs: a starting point.

The library is a bottomless well of ideas for illustrators. Probably there are two things I love most about using books for inspiration. The first is that it creates an emotional distance from the idea. Some people can just draw and draw, but I'm crippled by self-doubt unless I have a lot of confidence in the concept that I start with. I don't have to worry about whether James Joyce's ideas are good, so that lets me focus on agonizing over the pictures. It's incredibly liberating. It's also great practice for turning ideas into images. Illustrating isn't like drawing the view outside your window. You have to distill the concepts underlying the words and translate them into pictures, which is at least as challenging as the actual drawing.

So her grace o'malice kidsnapped up the jiminy Tristopher and into the shandy westerness she rain, rain, rain.

DAN AUGUSTINE

Dan Augustine describes his pen-and-ink drawings as "doodles"—things, he says, that aren't to be taken too seriously: "My first legitimate show was titled *A Series of Silly Doodles;* that's really what I do, little pen-and-ink sketches. Doodles. I don't take it tremendously seriously, because that just isn't me or my style."

Dan's work and attitude are an inspiration for people—grown-ups especially—who for whatever reason have stopped drawing or making art. His simple illustrations remind us of the joy in just drawing. "I just want my illustrations to make people smile, or giggle, or remind them of something, or take them back to someplace they remember."

Dan's show, *Everything is Fragile,* featured drawings of fifty of his favorite literary characters, from works like "Casey at the Bat" and *The Wind in the Willows.* "My work is made up of singular little moments in time, in most instances from a story, epic, or tale. . . . You don't get the full-length feature, you get just a little moment of the characters at their best or their worst."

02 21 31

☐ Use drawing or doodling as a new way of exploring a classic text. Try illustrating a character or a moment from Stevenson, Shakespeare, Vonnegut, or Bradbury.

☐ Group exercise: have each group member choose a classic text (the folklore section of your library should have many great examples) from which to read a chapter, scene, or poem aloud. Have other group members draw the scene as the reader reads.

☐ Hand-draw a "map" of your route to the library—it can be as simple as two points (your starting point and the library) connected by a line. Illustrate points you recall from that route, like storefronts, streetlamps, crosswalks, and other markers. Go for a walk while you're at the library; walk around a block or two, or up and down the street. Go back to the library and hand-draw your path from memory.

LAKE ALTOONA

Our House
(it's an octagon, no joke)

St. Mark's Church

Green Bar

Post office

New Library!

House w/ the Mickey Mouse garage doors

DIP in the road

Place where mom + I once drove off the road

Watch for crossing turkeys ...and deer

school grounds

Carolyn lived here

Trailer Court

ALTOONA

To Eau Claire

Gas station

Shane lived here

Way to the mall

Jenna lived here

[SO not to scale]

N W E

Between the Lines

LIBRARY COLLECTIONS ARE BURSTING WITH INSPIRING MATERIals that can spark creative ideas. This inspiration comes from the physical and digital collections we've already discussed, of course, but it also comes from the collection of people a library represents. In many ways, libraries are a microcosm of the communities they serve: in a single afternoon at a public library, for example, you're likely to see parents and children, seniors and students, job seekers and entrepreneurs, the well-to-do and the homeless.

If people watching sparks your curiosity and fuels your creative brain, a library is prime real estate, and not just because a broad cross section of people are represented there. Libraries are places where people share and find information, so they're also the perfect place to interact with many different kinds of people and glean new ideas and inspiration, just as you would by browsing through the books or music in your library's stacks. Author Brian P. Hall sees libraries as "a complete experience" because of this confluence of physical and experiential information.

BRIAN P. HALL

Brian Hall can't write without the library. "As a writer who relies on the works of others for inspiration, my relationship to libraries is essential," he says. "We—libraries and I—are allies, working together for the creative good."

Brian finds ideas for his projects in numerous, often disparate texts—stories, myths, and iconic books, to name a few. His piece "Study Bible: The Parable of Natural Law" is a perfect example of his far-ranging inspirations: it's laid out in columns like the classic Gideon Bibles you might find in a hotel room, but the text is a dark, metaphorical narrative that interweaves its exploration of the human condition with biblical passages.

> **WE—LIBRARIES AND I—ARE ALLIES, WORKING TOGETHER FOR THE CREATIVE GOOD.**

Brian's creative practice utilizes the library in a more complete fashion than simply discovering and reading other works. "I'm an intellectual grazer," he says. "At a library, I will walk around the stacks and pull books to read or skim. Sometimes I find inspiration in a passage. Sometimes I find it in a picture in an art collection. Sometimes the ramblings of a homeless man in front of the library could influence something I'm working on. It is a complete experience."

While this process may seem desultory, it's anything but. Brian deliberately places himself in the way of inspiration by frequenting his local library, and it's not just access to works of literature that draws him in. The library is useful to him and his writing not only as a resource, but also as a social space; his work pulls snippets of experience and inspiration together in a kind of literary collage, one that is richer, more nuanced, and more believable for the variety of influences that inform it.

Study Bible:
The Parable of Natural Law

Brian P. Hall

The Steeple's Clouds

45 Dear Friends, [a]I have spent the last fourteen mornings waking up in a hotel room full of people and bottles lying on their sides, dripping liquid from open mouths. [3]Though some look familiar, most, I have to admit, I don't remember meeting. [4]The first morning this happened I was frightened and tried to piece together the past night, but I was younger then. Immature. I've grown now. [5]I've learned to accept my place just the way it is. [6]And, so far, the only thing that has made me nervous is the vision. Or should I call it a memory? No, I'll call it a vision. I have had it every morning when I stand to search for my clothes.[d]

[7]In this vision, I'm sitting in the red, plush pew in my parents' church, a large evangelical chapel with a towering steeple that sticks clouds as they go by. At least, that's what I imagine because I'm at that age, 10 or 15 or 30, where church-

45:2-6
[d]2Pe2:2-1;Jude 4; 1Ti4:1; Ac10:42; 1 Ti 6:14; Gal 2:4; Tit 1:16; 1Cor10:14

45:7[e]Joel 2:28; Ac 2:17; Isa 11:2; Nu 11:17; Jn 7:37-39

45:8 [f]Pr 25:14

45:10 [g]Jude 12; 2 Pe2:13; 1 Cor 11:20-22; Eze 34:2,8,10; Eph 4:14; Mt 15:13

stuff—singing, dancing, praying, and speaking-in-tongues—is dull and boring, so I entertain myself by imagining clouds being ripped open by the church's steeple and zipping around the sky like rapidly deflating balloons.[e]

[8]When the airless clouds fall to earth, they land in trees, parks, and parking lots. Many people see these, essentially, dead clouds, but they don't recognize them as such because the clouds bear a close resemblance to used condoms—long tubes secreting some sort of condensation—so[f] [9]instead of picking up the clouds and saying, "Oh my god, I'm touching a cloud!" the usual response is something along the line of "Oh my god, don't touch that!" Unless, of course, [10]the ones finding them are from my parents' church because they'll say, "Oh, my God, please bless the sinners who defiled this parking lot," not realizing that they are, in fact, partly to blame because it was

☐ Spend an hour or two people watching at your library. Bring a sketchbook or notebook with you, and describe the different people you see as drawings or short character descriptions. Shoot for a variety of ages and types of people in your sketches. Consider how you might build a visual or written narrative around these people as characters. Imagine what they did this morning before coming to the library. Imagine what they're working on and why. Imagine where they would be if they weren't at the library, and why they would be there.

☐ If you're feeling chatty, strike up a conversation with a fellow library patron. Don't go into your conversation with a plan, but do try to focus on asking questions—find out a little bit about the person and see if what you learn fits your original drawing or description. If you're shy around strangers, remember that the librarians are there to help—even if it means just having a quick conversation!

☐ Sit in different areas of the library and listen to the sounds and conversations around you. Jot down snippets of conversations to use later in sketches, dialogue, and so forth. How are conversations different in the children's area than at the reference desk? What can you tell about a person (or a character) just by how they speak?

☐ Wander the shelves and find some fiction or nonfiction and at least one art compendium. Leaf through until you light upon something that strikes you in each book—a quote or an image, for example. Place these ideas in the context of your earlier sketches and conversation gathering. Consider how they all might be part of a single story—how do they fit together to reveal someone's character or drive the plot forward?

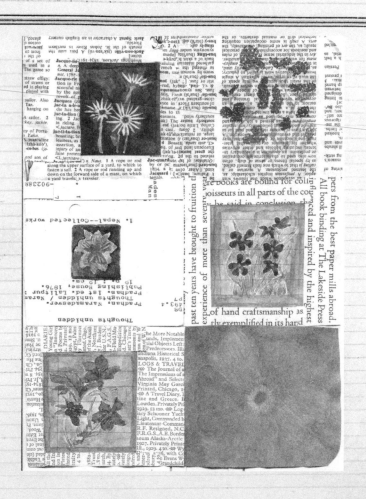

CHAPTER 3

Using the Library for Creative Research

C REATIVE PROJECTS CAN BE LIKE BUILDING PRO-
jects. They're both long-running, sometimes messy, and often delayed, but the
final results are usually impressive enough to make
the investment worth it: pieces that will be around
a long time and define a place or person. Both also
begin with a huge accretion of building materials.
In this case, we're talking about the books, articles,
objects, letters, documents, images, digitized texts,
and other resources that artists use to inspire and
inform their work.

New literary and historical interpretations,
social and scientific commentary, and even homages
to other works are the foundation of many artworks. To be truly effective, these kinds of creative
interpretations demand an accurate appraisal of
their source materials and references. Thorough
library research can help artists examine the context, point of view, and accuracy (or inaccuracy) of

a source work, which in turn can be a key factor in the ultimate success of their creative project.

In the examples that follow, we'll take a closer look at the research processes of a handful of artists working in paint and illustration, video and photography installations, poetry, plays, and dance in order to illuminate the ways in which the library can support in-depth creative research for long-running projects. Libraries not only provide access to a huge range of materials, but also to librarians, who are trained to be resources for any artist embarking on an in-depth project that requires research. Many librarians find that collaborating on research projects is the most rewarding part of their job, and artistic research partnerships, with their inherent flexibility and focus on discovery and inspiration, can be particularly fun.

Researching in Digital Collections

I N AN AGE OF GOOGLE BOOKS AND DIGITIZED ARCHIVAL AND
historical materials, digging into primary sources in the
course of creative research is easier than ever, and many
world-famous library collections that once required a research
grant to view are accessible online. Academic libraries in particular work to make new research and important historical
works available to as many people as possible, because open
access increases the opportunity for brilliant
scholarship and deeper, more nuanced under-
standings of science, history, and literature.

The arts are an important beneficiary of
library research and digital collections. Our
artist examples for this section are Nicola
Dickson and Kristen Baumliér, both of whom
use the library for in-depth research that
informs their artistic projects. Nicola's art is
ultimately a way to process and understand the
exploration and exoticization of her native
Australia, and to imaginatively engage with history. Kristen's
installations dig into controversial topics in science and history—most recently petroleum and mass food production—

> **"**
> LIBRARIES ARE
> CULTURAL INSTITU-
> TIONS WHERE ONE
> IS ABLE TO BOTH
> FACTUALLY AND
> IMAGINATIVELY
> EXPLORE THE PAST
> AND PRESENT
> **"**

to inform viewers, spur social change, and participate in a broader conversation about current events. Both of these artists' processes begin with library research, and are supported by new digital collections that make objects, images, and articles easier to find.

NICOLA DICKSON

"I am interested in how events and ideas of the past have influenced and persist within current cultural preoccupations," says Nicola Dickson, whose artistic process begins with in-depth historical research at the library. "Libraries are cultural institutions where one is able to both factually and imaginatively explore the past and present; I use their archives to provide resource material to develop imagery."

> *TO SEE HOW SOMETHING WAS MADE, TO IMAGINE WHAT MAY HAVE INSPIRED THE CREATOR, IS A VERY POTENT STIMULUS TO MY IMAGINATIVE ENGAGEMENT WITH THE PAST.*

Nicola's home library is the National Library of Australia, Canberra. At the start of a new project, she begins by searching the library's online catalog for material in the pictures collection. Then, she requests the originals she wishes to view in more detail so that she can document and respond to details that inform her concept and historical interpretation. A set of eighteenth-century jasperware medallions, made to commemorate the voyage of Captain Cook and the scientific records made during his exploratory voyage to Australia and Tasmania, inspired her *Wedgewood Blue Series.* The huge historical impact of these written and visual records in Britain and Europe fueled imperial expansion and colonization, so Nicola used similar imagery to comment on contemporary notions of Australia as a colony and a nation.

"My drawings refer to the fact that the wonder of novel plants, animals, and peoples became part of how Europeans interpreted and interacted with these regions and their indigenous peoples. Within my drawings, plant forms [recorded on the] Endeavour voyage transform and frame my translation of the portraits of Cook and Banks," says Nicola. "This body of drawings reminds the viewer of the labile and contested nature of Australian history."

For Nicola, library collections both inspire and inform her art, allowing her to not only learn about different historical eras, but also to handle historical objects directly. "To see how something was made, to imagine what may have inspired the creator, is a very potent stimulus to my imaginative engagement with the past."

━ EXERCISES

☐ Make an appointment with a reference or visual resource librarian to get the inside scoop on how to use digital collections. Use the same procedure outlined in Chapter 1: Exploring the Library as Subject, Exercise 1 on page 37.

☐ Browse a freely available digital collection (check the Resources list on page 199 for suggestions). Choose two to three images that catch your fancy and print them out. How would you recreate these images, or elements of them, in a different medium? What materials/format would you use? What are the soundtracks of these images? Write or draw some ideas on a notepad. Paste everything into a composition notebook or clip them together in an inspiration box for future exploration.

☐ Choose a time period or historic event and search the library catalog to find related titles, or ask a librarian for assistance. Look at the shelf for titles on the event or era you're interested in. If you can, choose one book on the topic that was published before 1950, and one that was published after 2005. Explore the books. Do the tables of contents touch on similar points? How does the writing about this event differ between the two books?

NOTE: If you have access to academic databases, try this exercise with scholarly articles on the same historic event or time period. Suggestions: the Roaring Twenties, the Gay Nineties, the Great Depression, the Dust Bowl, the Hundred Years' War, the London Blitz, and so on.

KRISTEN BAUMLIÉR

Kristen Baumliér's work explores issues in science and history in combined analog and digital pieces that incorporate video, sound, photography, performance, and installation. "I believe that art can communicate new ideas and call people to action," she says. "I see art-making as a process of research and discovery. . . . I find research to be exciting and an integral starting place for my projects."

It makes sense that Kristen uses libraries as a fundamental resource for developing the complex ideas in her work. She begins each new project by gathering as much information as she can on the topic her final piece will explore, using online search tools provided by her library to find books, images, and articles. Once the books she's requested come in, she spends time at the library looking at them, and also browsing the stacks. This added layer of serendipitous title discovery is also something she seeks out between projects, browsing new and featured book displays to find ideas and inspiration.

Her research spans academic, public, and special libraries and archives. At present, Kristen works at the Cleveland Institute of Art (CIA), where she has access to many libraries, each with its own collection focus and research space. "I often visit the Gund Library at CIA, which has a large collection of art and design books and one of the largest collections of artist books. I also use the Kelvin Smith Library at Case Western Reserve University, which has a variety of sitting and reading areas, and the Harold T. Clark Library at the Cleveland Museum of Natural History, which focuses on natural history books and resources. This past year, with my current work focusing on food and sustainability, I have been using the Cleveland Botanical Garden's Eleanor Squire Library. I also use the Cleveland Heights library, the Cuyahoga County library catalog, and have access to OhioLink, a network of 150 libraries across the state."

Kristen's research process is a playful, exhilarating one, and the performative aspect makes her gathering process part of the artwork itself. "I enjoy the 'hunt' and process of finding historical sources that are relevant to my projects. I also enjoy going to various libraries, and feel like the process is sometimes a performance in which I play the role of 'scholar' in search of information or new ideas."

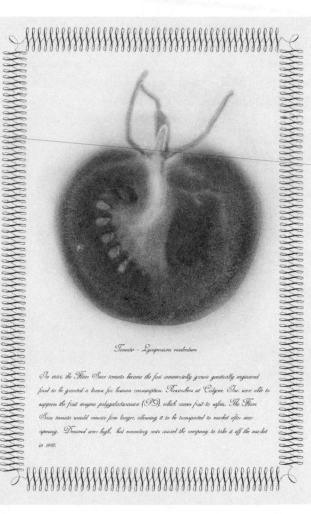

Tomato – Lycopersicon esculentum

In 1994, the Flavr Savr tomato became the first commercially grown genetically engineered food to be granted a license for human consumption. Researchers at Calgene, Inc. were able to suppress the fruit enzyme polygalacturonase (PG), which causes fruit to soften. The Flavr Savr tomato would remain firm longer, allowing it to be transported to market after vine-ripening. Demand was high, but mounting costs caused the company to take it off the market in 1997.

☐ Think of an issue that is important to you that has not yet been incorporated into your artistic process. Are you a vegetarian? Do you support cancer research, food banks, animal shelters, public television, or other political or charitable causes? These may seem like parts of your life that are separate from your work as an artist, but they require a level of commitment and concern that you can use in your work. Go to your library to gather information on a topic that's important to you. Dig into the history and the current issues surrounding that topic, including opposing viewpoints. Keep notes on the information, images, and perspectives you find in your search. Has your perspective deepened or changed as a result of your research? How can you communicate this complex understanding in your artistic work?

> *"*
> I ENJOY THE 'HUNT' AND PROCESS
> OF FINDING HISTORICAL SOURCES
> THAT ARE RELEVANT
> TO MY PROJECTS.
> *"*

☐ For many librarians, the opportunity to work with a patron on research questions that require a lot of collaboration is the best part of the job. If you're exploring a particular theme in your work, consider calling your local library to set up a meeting with a reference librarian. Bring your questions and ideas and talk about how you're gathering as much information, visual resources, and articles as possible. Ask for help, and communicate the timeline for your project (i.e., Will you want the librarian's help repeatedly throughout the process? Would you like a tutorial on how to search special databases? How long will you research before creating?) A research project like this can turn into a long-term collaboration.

NOTE: Be sure to acknowledge the librarian(s) who help you in artist's statements, notes, or appendices for your work!

Books, Books, Books

BOOKS ARE USUALLY THE FIRST THINGS THAT COME TO MIND when someone says, "library." Though libraries are much more than mere book warehouses, books remain important sources for artistic inspiration. Our next two artists rely on books, letters, and other documents to write their works, delving into library collections to research famous authors' lives and reinterpret them as art.

As a playwright reimagining Jane Austen for her play *Discovering Austen,* Kristin Hammargren immersed herself in the author's world, reading not only Austen's works, but also biographies, letters, and criticism. Research of this kind isn't only about establishing historical details and events, but also internalizing the personality and voice of an author whose works have had a huge impact on literature in the past two hundred years. Similarly, poet Rita Mae Reese researched Flannery O'Connor's life and work at a number of libraries and archives across the country in order to reimagine her life and respond to the themes in her work in a book-length series of poems.

Without the preservation efforts of libraries, original letters and documents—so evocative for creative work—would be lost.

KRISTIN HAMMARGREN

*D*iscovering Austen is a one-woman show Kristin Hammargren developed for her MFA thesis. The play is set in the dressing room of an actor who has been cast as Jane Austen in a play about the author's life. Before opening night, the actor is trying to answer her last nagging questions about who Jane Austen really was.

In a case of art mirroring life, this is much the same situation that Kristin found herself in when she began conducting research for *Discovering Austen*—though she'd loved the author ever since she read *Emma* as a girl, she knew little about Austen herself. "For all of the hundreds of books that have been written on Jane Austen, up to very recently, there has been some major misinformation," says Kristin. "Letters that her family edited, doctored pictures of her, et cetera. So, even though she died almost two hundred years ago, in some ways, scholarship about Austen is very new."

This means that people have interpreted Jane Austen differently at different times in history—a slippery problem for a playwright who wishes to create a believable character. Kristin's project demanded access to a wide range of books in order to build a nuanced characterization of Jane Austen and other characters in the final play; she not only read all of Jane Austen's books, but also used many biographies, minor works, criticism, and primary sources like letters and pictures.

"I tried to expose myself to all of the different interpretations of Austen and her work. Part of what I deal with in the play is how she is represented (or most often misrepresented) as a person, or even dumbed down as a writer, particularly in film adaptations."

To write the script, Kristin began by making a timeline of the events in Austen's life, and then wrote the first draft—essentially a biographical tale. "It was not very dramatic," she says. "My second draft became a little more like a play, but was still way too long. I had so much information and so many pieces from her writing that I wanted to include. . . . The fascinating part is that things I wrote twenty drafts ago and cut came back. The final script wove itself together from many different iterations going back over six months."

◄ EXERCISES

☐ Dive into the "words behind the words" of a favorite literary artist. Spend some time reading writers' published diaries and correspondence. Write a letter to a favorite writer (living or deceased) with news from your life. What would you say to him/her?

☐ Academic and public libraries often have audition guides, dialect tapes or CDs, and guides to developing performance resumes. Set up a meeting with a librarian to explore the options. He/she may be able to help you request materials from outside the library, depending on the materials that are available for checkout.

TIP: Public libraries frequently have large meeting spaces where open auditions can take place.

☐ Talk with your public or school librarian about hosting an audition or acting workshop for kids (and grown-ups!) in your community. Though many middle, high school, and community theater groups hold auditions, few people outside of theatrical circles know the ins and outs of formal (or even informal) auditions. Make sure to talk with the librarian well in advance to get on the programming schedule early.

RITA MAE REESE

"Most of what I've written (if not all) has been supported by time in the library," says Rita Mae Reese. The library, particularly the quiet workspace she finds at the University of Wisconsin–Madison's Memorial Library, is integral to her writing process. For one recent project, Rita Mae relied extensively on archival research to inform a discursive, poetic exploration of Flannery O'Conner's life. Many poems from the book, including the example here, begin with epigraphs from O'Connor's personal letters, highlighting how important library and archival source material was for the project.

If a poem is the product of a poet reorganizing what she knows, then Rita Mae's ideal library is the perfect reflection of how important libraries are to the artistic process. "I'm old-fashioned—I like the dusty old stacks, the tables, the quiet places. I'm also interested in the approach of a place of 'gentle chaos,' like the archive in San Francisco that shelves things by some arcane method so that you discover by searching. I wouldn't want the whole library to be like that, of course. But it might also make people appreciate all the order everywhere else."

Apocrypha:
Flannery and the Book of Tobit

Rita Mae Reese

That my stories scream to you that I have never consented to be in love with anybody is merely to prove that they are screaming an historical inaccuracy. I have God help me consented to this frequently.

—FLANNERY O'CONNOR TO BETTY HESTER, AUGUST 24, 1956

There are hundreds of ways to kill a husband
or a lover. There is a violence one soul
does to another, drawing and quartering
the beloved for a stupid remark, a lack
of talent, sentimental tastes. In the book of Tobit,
she finds Sara murdering her seven husbands,
one after the other on their wedding nights.
She is startled to see her own reflection
thousands of years away and ending
happily ever after, to find the demon
who drives her to violence cast out.
Each night she weaves her fingers together
until they ache, praying for a Tobias she won't destroy
to be led like a lamb into her newly tender hands.

 **EXERCISES**

☐ Rita Mae Reese believes that "the library is one of the surest cures for writer's block ever created. What better way to begin finding inspiration, or to learn writing techniques, than by reading and responding to great (and even not-so-great) literature?" Rita Mae uses primary sources to inform and inspire her poems. Responding to quotes, historical accounts, or letters you find at the library can be a great way to kick-start creativity.

☐ Do a little research: Learn about allusions, allegories, parodies, centos, and glosses—the ways in which poets and other artists often use primary source material to help them create new work, or to recall other works in reference to their own. Try your hand at incorporating some of these techniques into your own writing: Write a poem that responds to a famous line of poetry (William Carlos Williams's line, "It is difficult to get the news from poems . . ." is a good one), or incorporate references to other artists' work in a drawing.

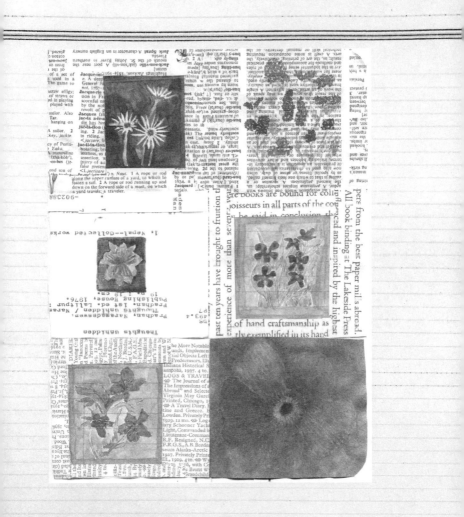

Digging into Multimedia

MANY ART FORMS ARE EASILY INCUBATED BY STANDARD library collections and spaces—poems and novels can be researched, written, and even performed in libraries; art and craft books are standbys for both print and digital collections, and special requests are easily ordered; three-dimensional works, two-dimensional works, and even more complex installations can be shown in library galleries and spaces.

When the artist in question is a performer, however, things get exciting! Performances—dance, theater, and music in particular—are special because they're ephemeral. Spend a week attending the same play each night, and you're sure to find that while the words and staging might be the same, the performance is not. The same might be said of dance or music. Part of the joy of experiencing and performing such art is that each instance is singular, and the connection between performer and audience is more exciting because it's fleeting.

This is all to say that a musician, dancer, or actor has the opportunity to dig into special multimedia collections, in addition to more traditional library resources, to incubate their art. Our artist example for this section is Christi Weindorf, who is both a dancer and a librarian. Her perspective on unique digital multimedia collections as a way to engage with the history of dance and inform her craft is a great template for performance artists who want to get more from their libraries.

NOTE: Be sure to check out the copyright section of the Resources list (page 199) for help on respecting copyright and using multimedia collections safely.

Christi Weindorf

Christi started dancing at age three, and became serious about pursuing dance as a career when she was a teenager. As an undergraduate student, Christi started choreographing and making dances. She also started teaching ballet classes and performing with a few small professional dance companies. After she received a BFA degree in ballet and modern dance, she worked in arts education and outreach, leading in-school artist residencies, teaching after-school dance programs, and coordinating lecture-demonstrations and performances.

Christi went on to earn an MA from Trinity Laban Conservatoire of Music and Dance in London, and more recently earned a degree in library and information science from San Jose State University in California.

As a teenager, Christi was (in her words) a "bunhead"—a major ballet nerd. "I wanted to learn everything I could about ballet, modern dance, theater, and all of the arts. I would go to the library to look up biographies on my favorite choreographers and performers, and then I would research the artists who inspired them.

"When I went to college, I was in love. There were so many books to read, so much to learn about, and so many people with ideas and opinions about dance, the arts, and life in general. I loved

> WHEN I WENT TO COLLEGE, I WAS IN LOVE. THERE WERE SO MANY BOOKS TO READ, SO MUCH TO LEARN ABOUT, AND SO MANY PEOPLE WITH IDEAS AND OPINIONS ABOUT DANCE, THE ARTS, AND LIFE IN GENERAL.

to spend time in the library with the dance journals from all over the world, looking at pictures and reading descriptions about contemporary dance in Europe. Access to videos was limited, as it still is, so I would read and imagine what these dances were like.

"During my MA studies at Laban, I practically lived in the library. The library was at the heart of the building, surrounded by studios and adjacent to the theater. In addition to doing research it was also the place to use computers, to edit videos, and to find a quiet place to work and write. It was where I could dig into the history and theories around contemporary dance in Europe.

"The library was instrumental in creating the final performance for my MA degree. I researched theater-directing techniques and applied that learning to direct dancers in the creation and execution of a performance. The library helped me to dig deep into the history and theories of the directors that I studied. I also used [the library] to study and try out different types of music with the work.

"When my work in dance education and performance started to feel unsustainable, I turned to a career in libraries. I knew that my love of teaching, research, and service to others that I had developed through my dance work would find a good home in a library setting."

Christi's ideal library is clearly influenced by the way she's used libraries in the past, channeling her own experience and research into an exciting multimedia space. "My ideal library would have access to millions of dance videos showing all kinds of dance works, historic and contemporary, popular and obscure. It would have video equipment for dancers to use, including editing software, and expert instructors to help with video production. The library would have physical and digital access to books and journals on a broad spectrum of topics related to dance, including theater, contemporary art, art history, communication, philosophy, critical studies, anatomy, kinesiology, physics, and more. It would also have videos and oral history recordings of artists discussing their work in choreography and performance. There are already libraries in existence that are more or less like this ideal described above.

"Another feature that would enhance an ideal library would be access to experts on a variety of dance topics, including dance training and repertoire. It would be amazing if libraries had experts on call who could teach or demonstrate various dance techniques or samples of choreography. So much dance knowledge and history is transmitted orally and through the kinesthetic experience of watching, trying, executing, and perfecting a movement or a series of movements."

For Christi, as both an artist and a librarian, preservation of past performances is a key concern. She discusses the importance of respecting the work and the artist when it comes to preservation: "My ideal library would be committed to preserving and providing access to dance performances. It would work with artists to find the best way to preserve each work in a way that fits the needs of the creators, the performers, and the performance. It would also provide access to performances on-site or nearby or through performance video screenings."

The library is a natural place for me to be drawn to, given that books serve as my primary inspiration. . . . And libraries are so much more than books too: the one near where I live now hosts classical music and dance performances, art exhibitions, art workshops, countless kids' activities. So, so much.

——CHERYL SONG

◀ EXERCISES

☐ Explore the holdings of a multimedia collection (see the Resources list for our favorites) and choose a video or audio recording to anchor you for the next few exercises. Take some notes while you watch/listen. How is your experience of this artwork or performance different than it might be in person? Consider the ephemeral nature of performed artworks. What is lost when you experience a recording of the work versus seeing it live? What is gained by having this material available in digital form?

☐ Create a responsive transcript of the work as you watch/listen. Draw or write your impressions as the performance happens; feel free to simply make free associations or to observe one aspect of the work (the sound of a poet breathing in between sentences, for example).

☐ Use your transcript to create a new artwork in your chosen medium, riffing on the themes, images, feelings, or other outstanding characteristics that you recorded while experiencing it. This can be a quick, sketched work or something more in-depth, depending on your engagement.

☐ Approach your art form by interrogating a different art form. Use the library to research and find information about another type of art. As you learn about this other type of art, what does it teach you about your usual medium? For example, how can a book about the history and appreciation of ceramics develop your eye for detail and inform the way you make dances? *

☐ Find books about games, particularly interactive, movement-based, and relatively simple children's games. Use a game or two as inspiration for creating movement and movement phrases. *

> ❝
>
> THE LIBRARY HELPED ME TO
> DIG DEEP INTO THE HISTORY
> AND THEORIES OF THE DIREC-
> TORS THAT I STUDIED. I ALSO
> USED IT TO STUDY AND TRY
> OUT DIFFERENT TYPES OF
> MUSIC WITH THE WORK.
>
> ❞

*Contributed by Christi Weindorf.

Scholarly Literature

S ANY ARTIST KNOWS, ART IS PART OF A LARGER CONVERSA-
tion. It can be political, educational, economical, or cultural, but the success of the work depends on how successfully it engages with that conversation. If you're creating an
installation that explores a scientific discovery, for instance,
and you don't read any of the reports about it, chances are your
work isn't going to make a meaningful statement.

This is where the library can help you dig into a different
kind of literature to find out more and inform your work. One
artist who knows the value of scholarly literature is Lisa Cinar,
an illustrator who's created an online shop full of creativity
kits for children. The success of her kits lies in how well they
help kids learn about basic art and storytelling techniques, like
color, design, and narrative. Because she wanted to contribute
something important to early childhood education, Lisa used
her library to learn how creativity develops and the theory and
practice of education.

Libraries everywhere are equipped with databases and
nonfiction sections (and helpful librarians!) that can help you
find scholarly literature, from articles and studies to long-form
books.

LISA CINAR

Lisa Cinar's art—and her business—were inspired and incubated by the libraries she used for research during grad school. "I think I first started to really discover the value of libraries during my studies at art school in Vancouver," she says. "I started doing research about children's picture books at the downtown Vancouver Public Library and was completely blown away when I walked into the children's section. I would spend hours just browsing."

Her early forays into children's illustration grew into a unique aesthetic and a business concept, and when Lisa first launched her shop, Draw Me a Lion, she knew she wanted her line of products to be fun and creative, but also have an important educational element. "I had formed my own notions about childhood and art and what would be important to pass on to children in my creations, but I wanted to know more about current ideas and philosophies when it came to early childhood education," she says. "I went straight to the library."

> *I STARTED DOING RESEARCH ABOUT CHILDREN'S PICTURE BOOKS AT THE DOWNTOWN VANCOUVER PUBLIC LIBRARY AND WAS COMPLETELY BLOWN AWAY WHEN I WALKED INTO THE CHILDREN'S SECTION. I WOULD SPEND HOURS JUST BROWSING.*

Lisa immersed herself in the scholarly works of Dewey, Montessori, Erikson, Piaget, and Vygotsky, and she started to understand the connections between today's Montessori and Waldorf educational systems and her personal observations on creativity and early childhood education. "It was important for me to know and learn about child development and early childhood education, since that is part of what I am trying to achieve with Draw Me A Lion."

If an artist is creating something that can be put into a category, Lisa believes "it is of tremendous importance to understand the history," but she also recommends keeping your research flexible and creative as you go along. "I like to do my research via the online library catalog first, and put the books that I think will be crucial to my new research or topic of interest on hold. However, when I come to pick up the books, I like to leave myself adequate time to browse through sections to find something extra via one of my favorite search methods—chance."

◆ EXERCISES

☐ Think about what you're trying to communicate in your work. Do your ideas engage with a broader category of research, like science, philosophy, or politics? Take some time to jot down the larger conversations related to your art.

☐ Choose one category from the list you made in Exercise 1 and spend a few moments fleshing out the specific conversation you want your art to engage. Write down everything you know about the topic, and record any questions you have, including areas of the conversation you don't know much about. Use your library to help you answer some of these questions. Search library databases for articles, the library catalog for books, or ask your librarian for help.

☐ Consider how your perspective has changed or deepened in response to your research. Sketch or write out ideas for a new piece that responds to the answers you were able to find to your questions at the library.

CHAPTER 4

*Using the Library
as a
Space to Work*

W E'VE HAD A CHANCE TO EXPLORE THE
conceptual business of the library in
the first three chapters—as space and
as a collection. In Chapter 4, we look at the library
as a community resource and offer some practical
ways you can incorporate your local library into
your creative working life.

First we take a look at the library as workspace.
Libraries have long functioned as workspaces for
people in all types of fields. For many writers, a
library is basically an office; it's open when you need
it (although one of our writers did lament the fact
that public libraries aren't open twenty-four hours a
day), it has computer stations and places to plug in
laptops, and it's generally a place where you're guar-
anteed some level of quiet.

The wonderful thing about libraries is that they
can accommodate the needs of many types of artists.
In the second part of this chapter, we examine the

library as a place to develop one's art through collaboration and new skill practice, through workshops and hands-on activities.

Using the Library as a Workspace

NOVELIST MADELEINE ROUX HAD A DEADLINE FROM HER publisher looming when her personal laptop died. Her solution? Head to the library on the Beloit College campus in Beloit, Wisconsin.

"Completing my sequel could have been much more difficult, but I had a cozy, quiet place to work, a little home away from home for a few weeks. It's hard to say if it inspired part of the novel, but just having that peaceful atmosphere is invaluable to a writer."

The work of writing is usually a solitary pursuit. For many writers (even those with functional laptops), the public or university library offers a midpoint between a quiet office and a bustling public space—we affectionately refer to this as the "kitchen effect" (the phenomenon wherein people gravitate to the kitchen, even to work independently, to be in the presence of others). You may find a similar effect at a coffee shop or bookstore, but the library provides a no-charge option, plus ample opportunity for tackling creativity fatigue, as we've seen in previous chapters.

Even if you already have a favorite writing spot, a change of scene can do wonders for productivity and can help combat writer's block. Try incorporating your public library into your daily or weekly writing rhythm, perhaps by sitting and writing at one of the study tables for two hours every Saturday.

Do you already do your best writing in your library? Make the most of your time there by using the collection to take a mental break. Spend half an hour reading something completely unrelated to the project you're working on. Explore the library's book displays and book lists, or chat with a librarian to get reading recommendations. Plunge into the genre areas of your library (westerns, romance, mysteries, science fiction), pick out the most outrageous and "unlike you" title you can find, and read the first chapter. What can you learn about your own work from a different kind of writing? How is the writing style of the book you chose effective or ineffective for the story?

Some libraries also function as studio spaces for visual artists, digital artists, musicians, and craftspeople, whether as a "third space" away from both home and office, or as a convenient place to get some work done while traveling. These studios may take a variety of forms, from a digital media center (where users can work with equipment to produce films, audio, and more) to a worktable where users can make and share craft and other art projects. The Minneapolis Central Library not only has an extensive sheet music collection, but also a piano room

> " COMPLETING MY SEQUEL COULD HAVE BEEN MUCH MORE DIFFICULT, BUT I HAD A COZY, QUIET PLACE TO WORK, A LITTLE HOME AWAY FROM HOME FOR A FEW WEEKS. IT'S HARD TO SAY IF IT INSPIRED PART OF THE NOVEL, BUT JUST HAVING THAT PEACEFUL ATMOSPHERE IS INVALUABLE TO A WRITER. "

that patrons can book for private lessons or practice time. Some libraries even have guitars and other portable instruments available for checkout! On the more technical end of the spectrum, Brooklyn Public Library's Shelby White and Leon Levy Information Commons offers a range of studio spaces for traditional and digital projects that community members can use. Studio spaces for film and music production, complete with lighting, green screens, sound-editing software, and a variety of other tools are all available through the Info Commons; workshops and tutorials complement the new space and give people the opportunity to learn to use new equipment and technology for their creative projects. Such high-tech spaces are wonderful resources for creative types who don't have the room or the money to outfit their house with studio spaces.

The "studio" space does not have to look like a typical artist's studio, as Nathan Yeager's library drawing group demonstrates. Nathan is a resident of Gig Harbor, Washington, a public library patron, and an artist with a day job. He wanted a place in Gig Harbor where he could practice his art with other artists, at a time that worked with his schedule. He approached the library and worked with staff there to book the library's public meeting room on a regular basis so that he and other hobbyists could get together to practice their art in a "just formal enough" setting. The library did not need to provide drawing instructors or drawing supplies—just space.

Traveling can sometimes put a cramp in your creative style, especially when you're on the road for long stretches of time, or if you just don't have a lot of room in which to work when you're on a trip. Luckily most communities have a public library that by its very nature is open and available to all, even out-of-town visitors! Stop by the library to see what kind of workspace is available, and set up shop on a free afternoon. Let library staff know that you're visiting and are looking for a quiet place to work—they may be able to tell you about rooms you can reserve, computer policies for visitors, and more.

Does your community have an art supply swap? Some libraries host these events, where artists bring (gently) used or excess art supplies to share and trade with each other. If you're interested in this type of program, ask to speak with the librarian or staff person in charge of programming. You can also read more in Chapter 6 about how to create a successful programming partnership with your library.

Using the Library to Learn or Practice a New Skill

Even more than books, the [library] is made of people.
It is one of the last truly social resources left that anyone uses.
—WENDY MACNAUGHTON, 2013 INTERVIEW

L IBRARIES AREN'T JUST FOR THOSE SEEKING QUIET SOLITUDE—
if you crave the social part of creation, you can find it in
library workshops and programs. Even if you're working on an individual project, being part of a group means you
can take advantage of the collective skills you all bring to the
table. You can ask for help with a particularly tricky technique,
bounce ideas off other workshop participants, and offer your
own expertise.

Libraries may play one of two roles when it comes to
workshops. Workshops may be held in library space and facilitated by outside partners (e.g., a local artist or writer), or
workshops may be facilitated by the library itself (e.g., by a
library staff member or by someone closely affiliated with the
library such as a Friends group or library board member).

Libraries post notices about workshops and programs in a variety of ways—from social media, to online calendars, to community bulletin boards. If you can't find a calendar of events easily on your library's website or at the library itself, ask a staff member to point you in the right direction.

WORKSHOPS FOR WRITERS Many libraries are the home for writing critique groups (check the programming calendar to see if these groups are accepting new members), where members can receive and offer feedback on their work. Libraries may also host hands-on workshops with professional writers and creative writing educators.

Check your library's program calendar or ask one of the staff members if the library hosts any workshops or programs related to National Novel Writing Month, or NaNoWriMo. This annual novel-writing project is a great way to connect with new and experienced writers (known as "Wrimos") across the country and, increasingly, the world. Many libraries host special NaNoWriMo programs like write-ins and writeathons, and support programs through NaNoWriMo's library program, Come Write In.

WORKSHOPS FOR PERFORMERS Though less prevalent than workshops for writers, some libraries do serve as workshop or class space for different kinds of performers. Types of workshops include audition how-tos (some theater groups hold the actual auditions in libraries), basic acting and dance or movement workshops, reader's theater, and poetry readings or slam poetry.

WORKSHOPS FOR VISUAL ARTISTS Many libraries host workshops or guided studio time for visual/digital artists and craftspeople, facilitated by professional artists, hobbyists, and art educators. These workshops offer a structured time to learn a new technique and ask questions of instructors and other workshop participants. They're also a way to get to know people in your community.

Art-making workshops (visual, writing, or performance), including those in a field or technique in which you're not an expert, are a great excuse and opportunity to work outside of "your" art. Practicing a new or unfamiliar creative skill can actually help spark new ideas and create new connections when it comes to your own creative practice.

With their informal structure and no/low cost, library programs and workshops are a fantastic way for artists and makers of all kinds to learn new techniques and connect with others in a low-pressure environment. We love this kind of workshop because it gives participants a chance to try out new kinds of art-making without shelling out a lot of money for a formal art class.

NOTE: Are you a writer, performer, or instructor looking for a place to hold workshops? Check with your local library to see if you can reserve a meeting or program room (these are typically available for free or very low cost), especially if workshop or rehearsal space is at a premium in your community. See Chapter 6: Creating Successful Programming Partnerships with Libraries, for additional information on best practices for working with your library.

CHAPTER 5

Using the Library as an Arts Venue

AT THEIR CORE, LIBRARIES ARE ALL ABOUT PROVID-
ing free, democratic access to information.
Think about the art you create: Isn't it
information? Can you feel a sweeping sense of narrative and emotion—just as you do when you read
a book—when you look at a painting or watch a
film? When you compose music or write a new play,
your work is part of the whole canon of music and
plays through history. Chances are, no matter what
kind of art you make, you reference other works
that have influenced you in each piece you create;
you build upon or refute the ideas and themes that
were put forth in the art that came before.

Ideas, themes, narrative, emotion, history—this
stuff is information. And libraries are committed to
sharing information freely with anyone who wants
it, so communities and people can function in society as informed entities and lead richer, more connected lives. Artists' work is part of this information

landscape, and the library is the ideal place to share it with the world. In many ways, the library is already an arts venue, given the kinds of information it shares and its place at the center of the community, open to all different people. Why wouldn't a place like that want to share new work, live and in person?

Libraries regularly hold readings of new poetry and fiction, workshops that aim to teach the craft of writing, and book festivals to celebrate writers, both local and national. Libraries show new work by unknown artists, school groups, and locals, and they do it in every kind of gallery space, from small glass cases, to reading room track mounts, to room-size installations. Libraries serve as performance spaces for new theater that brings literature to life, and music that can bring people together.

In each case, the library offers one of the most important commodities for any artist: an audience. And not just any audience—an audience of every kind of person in the community. Free access for all means that the people who come to the library are young and old, rich and poor, unemployed and nine-to-fivers, and every race, color, and creed. At the library, everyone will be able to see your work and respond to it, love it, or hate it. Your work will be part of their lives at the library, even if for just a moment.

Author Readings, Signings, and Festivals

LIBRARIES ARE ALREADY GOOD AT SHOWCASING THE WORK OF writers, so it should come as no surprise that your library is an ideal venue for a variety of events that promote new works of poetry, fiction, and nonfiction. Readings, book signings, and literary festivals all take place at libraries.

Some libraries, like the Princeton Public Library in Princeton, New Jersey, are go-to book tour stops for internationally known authors, blending the larger international publishing scene with local authors for truly egalitarian programs that can introduce patrons to a lot of new and exciting work.

Poets are especially well-served by libraries; they are a place to hold open mics, to schedule mini book tours for new chapbooks or collections, or to hold monthly writing workshops. Writers who partner with libraries can help librarians create workshops for children or teens, or help build a suite of programs in honor of National Poetry Month. The possibilities are endless.

Dr. Michael Salcman, our example for this section, runs a prominent literary group in Baltimore, and their events are all hosted at the Main Branch of the Enoch Pratt Free Library in downtown Baltimore—a place that is inspirational not only for its architecture and vast collection, but also for its democratic openness. Meeting or reading in libraries is not only free, but also a great way to share your work openly, with many different people—not just folks who are part of your scene.

Michael Salcman

In a life comprised of many kinds of research and writing—from the highly technical to the artistic—Michael Salcman has spent a good deal of time in libraries. "As my medical career wound down, I broke a ten-year literary silence and started writing poetry again," he says. "The libraries of my life provided an environment that inspired me and made me want to have my own books of poetry greeting people as they entered."

For a neuroscientist who calls the brain "a metaphor-making machine," libraries serve not only as inspiration, but also as a venue for experiencing and sharing new work. "Libraries inspire me with the combination of visual art wed to an encyclopedic storehouse of information," Michael says. The architecture of his favorite libraries; the democratic philosophy; and the sheer number of interesting books, magazines, and artworks, allows his work to reference art, culture, and science broadly and to comment on the human condition with precise metaphors.

> " YOUR LIBRARY IS AN IDEAL VENUE FOR A VARIETY OF EVENTS THAT PROMOTE AND SPOTLIGHT THE WORK OF POETS AND WRITERS. "

The library also provides a place to share his poems with others. "I give poetry readings and lectures on art and the brain in libraries; my favorite local libraries include the small and elegant Roland Park Branch of the Enoch Pratt Free Library near my home, and the Main Branch in downtown Baltimore, where we hold the CityLit Festival every year. The Main Branch has a room devoted to poetry and the relics of its namesake, Edgar Allan Poe."

As he says, a library isn't just a place to find models for your own writing, it's also "a place to go to hear poetry and literary fiction read, to hear art. A library is a unique and beautiful place to hold meetings of writers and artists and to promote reading and writing in the general population."

The Dog Speaks

Michael Salcman

—INTERIOR WITH DOG BY MATISSE, 1934

I'm only half-asleep so I know you're standing there
wondering if I'm asleep. Nope.
It's not easy to rest under this table—
for one thing, there's a strong downward slope
and gravity's got me half tipped out of my basket
like an apple by Cézanne.
Talk about a flat world!
For another, I can't get away from these colors,
the red floor tiles, orange table leg
and pink wall burning on my lids like the sun.
Then again I'm never alone; the kids think a gray dog is cute
and I'm the only dog in the room. I was bribed
(that's my excuse) with a bone
and a bowl of fresh water. Really,
I wish you wouldn't stare—it's extra hard to be an icon
when you're not an odalisque and have no hair.
Here's the inside dope, he wore a vest when he painted *them*
but saved his housecoat for *me*. I liked sitting for him,
he was never rude and spared me his violin.
I think I look very dignified, not naked, just nude.

Cutting Apples
Michael Salcman

My Father always carried a penknife
to pare his green apples, raising their skins
in perfect spirals. He never drew blood
slicing his bananas for breakfast,
their dark-seeded cores like little faces
dropping into the milk, one more item
in a life of a thousand chores,
one more notch in a life advancing
by millimeters or inches, not seconds or days.
I watched him turn himself as carefully away
from violence as a lathe on a table leg,
cutting each curve and flourish
from the flat face of a block
clamped in his hand. His hand and its thumb
never shied from the blade; he knew
that what you do with any tool gives it its value,
like a life—not too eager or afraid.

Galleries and Exhibitions

Libraries can be a wonderful place to showcase artwork and share your work with a huge cross section of people. Many of the artists who've done interviews with the Library as Incubator Project see library galleries and shows as a prime opportunity to connect with people in their community and to reach a much broader audience than they could in a traditional gallery space or a museum show.

We're certainly not knocking those venues—galleries and museums contribute a lot to communities!—but libraries, especially public libraries, offer a rare opportunity to show work where everyone in the community can access it. The cost of visiting certain venues, like upscale galleries and museums, can be prohibitive for students, people with lower incomes, or people with little kids. Not so at the library.

Libraries are also usually more open to hosting the work of local artists, artists who are just starting out, and folks whose work is less high art and more craft—qualities that Trent Miller, our next artist example, sees as tremendously important for both artists and communities of potential art appreciators. Librarians see the library as a necessary showcase for art—they see it as a way to share another kind of information, just like the information in books, articles, and DVDs—and they often have a network of local contacts to help them fill their gallery spaces, if they have them. Spaces can range from glass display cases, to professional track mounting for the walls and exhibition space for larger works, to simple cork boards where work can be hung with tacks, but the end result is the same: more people viewing new art.

TRENT MILLER

Trent Miller is an artist who works in a library. As you might expect, the library influences his painting, but his work as an artist also influences his library work. Trent's many contacts in the art world help keep the gallery space at the Madison Public Library's central location buzzing.

In his time at Central, the library has shown a range of well-known artists, and artists who are just starting out. Trent says his favorite thing about the library as gallery space is that it provides people access to art that wouldn't be found in a museum, and gives patrons who might not go to a commercial gallery a chance to enjoy art in person.

One early 2011 show, *The Beast in Me*, which Trent curated with his wife, poet J. L. Conrad, brought in artwork by graduate students from the Art Department of the University of Wisconsin–Madison. The show received a great response from the public, and allowed the graduate students, who'd never shown in a library before, to interact with a broad range of people from the community, most of whom they never would have met without the common space of the library. Creating these connections—between art, the people who make it, and people in the community—is what excites Trent about his work as gallery coordinator.

"I have worked in libraries for about ten years now," he says. "I got my first library job as a teen librarian because of my background in art education. I like the library environment and feel that it mixes well with being an artist. I am always exploring new ideas; for me libraries are an amazing source of free knowledge and source material. I can investigate as much as I want and the price is free!"

In his ideal library, this investigation would include art and art-making techniques made freely available within the open community space of the library. "I think that these kinds of collaborative spaces speak to the idea of incubator," he says.

In Trent Miller's ideal library, you'll find:

- A nice gallery space for paintings, drawings, and other two-dimensional work
- A designated space for installation, three-dimensional, and video work
- An art checkout program for customers
- A community workspace for artists to use within the library

Trent actively works to make his own library more useful and accessible to artists by developing a consistently strong and organized gallery schedule to serve both artists and the public, and by working to incorporate more hands-on learning experiences into library spaces and the programs he coordinates.

PERFORMANCE SPACES

Many libraries are equipped with small performance areas used for public meetings and events and children's story-time programs. These spaces run the gamut from formal theater spaces to pop-up stages, and from multifunction meeting rooms to an unassuming corner of the stacks with a few chairs.

Don't expect effects or lighting, but do expect the audience to be an exciting mix of people who want to see something new, or who have never seen a live performance before, regardless of the genre. Whatever the available space, a little work and creativity can transform a library into a dynamic stage, and it can be an ideal stage for a performer who wants to share his work with a broad range of people—not just fans or people "in the know." In this way, the library can be a powerful tool for outreach and information, connecting people with important ideas and new and exciting performances, and offering an important platform for conversations about politics, art, and social issues. Brandon Monokian, a theater artist, found a home for his performance work at the Princeton Public Library as he searched for a way to respond to all of these needs in his work.

> " WHATEVER THE AVAILABLE SPACE, A LITTLE WORK AND CREATIVITY CAN TRANSFORM A LIBRARY INTO A DYNAMIC STAGE. "

BRANDON MONOKIAN

When we asked Brandon Monokian how libraries have informed his work, his response was surprising and exciting: "When I first started studying theater in college, I never imagined my work would lead me to doing theater in places that were not theaters; now it is my preference."

Brandon's artistic relationship with libraries—Princeton Public Library in particular—started with a book challenge: *Revolutionary Voices: A Multicultural Queer Youth Anthology* was removed from the high school and public library in his hometown after a small group of activists began targeting the books on the Gay, Lesbian and Straight Education Network's reading list. "In protest of the book's removal, I worked with a group of theater artists and activists to create Revolutionary Readings," Brandon says. "We toured the New York and New Jersey area, performing readings from the book," a project that eventually led to the Princeton Public Library and a performance during Banned Books Week. "From there, I began work with librarian Janie Hermann to create the Page to Stage program, a performance series featuring staged readings of plays that have been adapted from or inspired by literature."

Page to Stage is an ongoing collaboration at the Princeton Public Library in New Jersey; Brandon facilitates the production

> **I NEVER IMAGINED MY WORK WOULD LEAD ME TO DOING THEATER IN PLACES THAT WERE NOT THEATERS; NOW IT IS MY PREFERENCE.**

of short plays performed by young adults, and the shows are open to the public as library events. "Tying live theatrical entertainment to literature serves as an animated way to promote literacy," Brandon says. He believes that doing theater in a library can accomplish a library's goals—goals that aren't usually achieved through traditional theater—and can be an important political statement in addition to a creative collaboration. "It's a way to show how useful theater is to society, especially when we see the arts on the budget chopping block so often."

Working in nontheater spaces has also challenged Brandon creatively. "When I did Sarah Ruhl's *Eurydice* for the Page to Stage series, the play called for a river onstage. Our river became a massive collection of recycled water bottles." To create the right atmosphere for another play without any special lighting or effects, Brandon turned to a local band called Spinner's End; now they often work together to score theater productions. "Because of spatial and technical limitations at the library, my creative mind has been pushed to new places; I couldn't be happier."

MAKE IT WORK FOR YOU

At the Library as Incubator Project, we believe a library isn't just about things like books, databases, magazines, and free tax forms—it's also about people. People like librarians, who are trained to find the right information for a patron from the massive sea that's easily available, both in print and online. A library, to us, is about people and skills; it's a place to connect and create.

At a time when arts organizations and libraries are both suffering from slash-and-burn budget cuts, creating partnerships between them is a sound way to weather the storm, share resources, and work from a place of strength in the community to advocate for both libraries and arts. As an artist, you can reach out to your local libraries to make connections and further the practice of, and publicity for, your art.

> " WE BELIEVE A LIBRARY ISN'T JUST ABOUT THINGS LIKE BOOKS, DATABASES, MAGAZINES, AND FREE TAX FORMS— IT'S ALSO ABOUT PEOPLE. "

REACHING OUT TO YOUR LOCAL LIBRARY

FINDING THE LIBRARIES IN YOUR AREA If you want to use the library to help promote your work, do it the courtesy of becoming a regular patron if you aren't already. Learn how to use your library's spaces and resources through the exercises we've outlined in previous chapters, and get to know the people. A partnership is a relationship, and that means give and take on both sides. If you treat your library and your librarians as partners, everyone wins!

ADVICE ON DEVELOPING A LIBRARY-FRIENDLY PROGRAM As we've said before, librarians are an overworked lot. They're often excited about great programming ideas, but swamped by other duties and concerns like shrinking budgets. If you plan ahead and develop a relationship with a librarian at your library, you have a much better chance of forming a lasting, mutually beneficial program.

Some things to consider:

1 Librarians often do monthly themes for programming and events based on the American Library Association (ALA) calendar. The ALA website often has great kits for quick programming and marketing that are go-tos for librarians who need to plan a year's worth of events on a minimal

budget. Take a look around the ALA website for events like Teen Read Week, history celebrations like Black History Month, and so on. Consider how your work could fit into these themes.

2   Local events are also good to know about. If your city does an annual arts or cultural festival or has a rich local tradition, consider how your art could be incorporated into that idea to help the library celebrate.

3   Consider how your art could be taught to many different age groups or disciplines. You may be excited to teach adults how to paint, but the librarians may need someone to develop a teen program. Be flexible.

4   Think about cost. If you can plan a program that costs very little (or nothing!), you have a better chance of working with a library. Don't expect to get a stipend (though you might get lucky); instead, consider the nonmonetary benefits of volunteering your time and work at the library. You'll be building good connections with a lot of people who want to know about your work.

5   Brainstorm ways that your program could become a suite of services. If you want to show your paintings in the library's gallery, consider how you might supplement that show in order to both serve the library *and* broaden the reach of your show. If you host a workshop or series of

workshops on painting during the month that your show is up, and you work with a librarian to create a display of library resources related to painting, you're not only marketing your work, sharing your expertise with the community, and creating interest in yourself as a community artist, you're also providing the library with three services that don't require much legwork on their part.

6 Consider timing. Many libraries plan programs anywhere from six months to two years in advance. Creating a partnership with your librarians will help you become a resource for future programming. Start small, then go for broke.

Programming Ideas

1 Host a writing/painting/acting/songwriting/video editing/et cetera workshop (or series of workshops) for kids, teens, or adults.

2 Partner with a collection development librarian to build a book display about your art for a celebration like National Poetry Month.

3 Create an art show, reading, or performance at the library.

4 Host a kid's story time or other activity to teach children about your genre/art.

5 Show your work in a library gallery space. Remember, you'll probably have to hang your own work!

Advice on Pitching Your Program

If you work with a librarian to learn what their programming needs are, you're already halfway there!

1 Have a plan, but make sure it's flexible.
   • Build on previous workshops you've run successfully at other venues. Libraries don't have the resources to launch something that might not resonate with their patrons.
   • Have a target age group for your program.
   • Have an ideal range of participants in mind (e.g., 5–15).

2 Outline space and material needs for the program.

- **SPACE:** What kind of room? How large?
- **MATERIALS:** What will you be making? Will the library be expected to provide materials, or will participants bring their own (in the case of a writing workshop, the library usually just has to find space).
- **COST ESTIMATE:** Bring a list of estimated prices for materials (if any); don't expect to get a stipend, but do have a modest number in mind based on other events you've done, in case someone suggests it.
- **EQUIPMENT:** Do you need a projector, laptop, or some other piece of equipment? What will you be bringing with you? It's a great idea to do a trial run a day or two in advance to make sure your tech works properly.
- **MARKETING PLAN:** Have a list of promotional ideas prepared in advance. Most libraries have marketing plans in place, even if they're sparse, but that doesn't mean they won't appreciate your input. Ask how your ideas might fit into their plans and budget. Suggest cross promotion for the event through your own social media networks.

CHAPTER 6

Creating Successful Programming Partnerships with Libraries

PRACTICING ARTISTS, ART EDUCATORS, AND ARTS organization leaders will find that library staff can be enthusiastic and important partners when it comes to promoting arts in communities of all sizes and makeups.

Partnerships with libraries mean that people of all ages and from all backgrounds have the opportunity to explore the arts in a comfortable and familiar environment. Libraries frequently function as venues for arts groups (see Chapter 5 for details on how to pursue partnerships like this in your community). This chapter outlines examples of, and ideas for, partnerships that connect the library to the arts community on levels that expand on the idea of library as venue.

First we look at ways that existing organizations (such as artist co-ops, community theaters, and more) can partner with their local library to enhance engagement in the arts in their community.

Then we talk about "one-off" or special program planning and development—those one-time events (anything from author readings to guest story-time presenters) require careful planning ahead of time. Lastly, we take a look at ways organizers of large-scale, multifaceted programs (National Novel Writing Month, book or film festivals, and so on) can work with their local libraries to incorporate them as satellite venues.

Partnerships for Existing Organizations

ARE YOU AN ACTIVE MEMBER OF AN ARTS ORGANIZATION IN your community? Maybe it's a visual arts cooperative, or a community theater, or the local symphony orchestra. Working with your local library can create a fantastic outreach program that will do the following:

- Engage more people (including hard-to-reach populations) with community arts

- Offer a space for free or low-cost promotion of upcoming performances, auditions, events, or classes

- Provide a way to interact directly with your community audience, hear their thoughts and ideas about the work you do, and communicate your organization's message

> " BY . . . MAKING ARTISTS A PERMANENT FIXTURE IN THE LIBRARY ARENA, AWARENESS OF THE ARTS WILL BECOME MORE PREVALENT. "

One example is the close partnership between the Fond du Lac Visual Arts collective (FDL Visual Arts) and the Fond du Lac Public Library in Fond du Lac, Wisconsin. The formal partnership between these two organizations answered a need on both sides. FDL Visual Arts needed a place to hold continual exhibitions of their members' work, while the library had a gallery that needed to be filled and maintained. In November 2010, the partnership became official. FDL Visual Arts now curates the Langdon Divers Gallery at the library's main branch, and is an integral part of the library's operation.

Melissa Kolstad is a collagist/ephemeralist who works closely with the Fond du Lac Public Library as a member of the FDL Visual Arts collective. She echoes many of our ideas about arts, community, and the role of libraries in the support of both.

> By . . . making artists a permanent fixture in the library arena, awareness of the arts will become more prevalent. This is especially necessary in rural areas. When a community is surrounded by art, acceptance of all types of art will happen more readily, and in turn, more children will be exposed to the fine arts. It's a win-win for everyone involved, especially as arts programs are being cut from school budgets.

Tips for Long-Term Partnerships

Research: Check out your library's website to see if there's any information on the topic of community organization or library partnerships. Set up an "exploratory" meeting with a person from your library to discuss a potential partnership (when scheduling the meeting, ask for the person in charge of community outreach, partnerships, and/or programming). Even a thirty-minute meeting means the library staff member is able to devote his/her attention to the topic for half an hour rather than being caught between desk shifts, program prep, computer assistance, and other duties. Come to the meeting with ideas for what the partnership might mean, but be ready to brainstorm with the library staff person too—he/she will have a good sense of the kinds of programs and partnerships that have worked in the past.

Communication: Is this a formal arrangement, where both parties agree to a set of regular responsibilities (e.g., an arts organization agrees to take over curation of a library gallery), or is it more casual (e.g., there's an understanding that the library can contact organization members to do artist demonstrations or workshops)? If the former, you may want to consider drafting an agreement that both parties can sign.

Connection: Consider making one person from the library and one person from the arts organization the liaisons for the partnership. For example, the Fond du Lac Public Library has a community liaison who works with local organizations and individuals. This helps streamline communications and means that questions can be answered more efficiently.

NOTE FOR LIBRARIES: Please consider putting the contact information for this person on your library website!

One-Off/Special Program Planning and Development

Libraries are excellent venues for one-time programs conducted by local groups, but the one-off nature of these programs means that groups or individuals from farther afield can participate too.

These special programs are often part of a larger initiative like the following:

- A summer reading program;

- A community "Big Read" or common reading program;

- A community centennial or other local celebration;

- A program series related to a specific topic (e.g., live music, knitting, visual arts, storytelling),

or they may simply be part of the library's programming schedule. An example of a special or one-off library program is found in Playbods, a Leeds, England—based artist duo that brings hands-on art workshops for kids into public libraries.

Playbods is a collaboration between two established Leeds artists: Bryony Pritchard, a visual artist and performer, and Kim Glassby, a dance and movement artist. Both artists aim to deliver playful, multisensory, interactive performances and projects to community groups and individuals of all ages, abilities, and backgrounds. In this collaboration, they're interested in how to engage the public in sensory play and interactive learning in the library environment, and how this impacts the way people feel within the library and enhances their interactions with the space and one another. Their programs are based on children's literature, but include games, art-making, and movement activities that extend elements of the stories they read.

When asked why they wanted to work with libraries in particular (as opposed to a community center or arts center), Bryony responded: "We loved the idea of bringing dance and creativity to places which are unexpected yet very public, and we were keen to break the conventions of libraries and explore how you could make libraries more relaxing and stimulating— places to celebrate stories in active and experiential ways."

Bryony and Kim approached several libraries with their idea, and the program was given the green light after the duo received funding from a Leeds granting board to cover the cost of supplies and time.

ONE-TIME PROGRAMMING IDEAS

- Arts workshops
- Themed book displays
- Readings or performances
- Children's story-time hour
- Art exhibition

(For a complete list of one-time program ideas, as well as tips on creating such programs, see Chapter 5, page 159.)

Tips for Planning One-Off/Special Programs

RESEARCH: Just like with the partnership section, it's important to plan ahead when approaching a library about a special program. As we've said previously, libraries tend to book their programming schedule months in advance—even earlier when it comes to scheduling entertainers and programs for their summer reading programs—so make sure you check in well ahead of when you'd like to do the program, or that your program is one that can be scheduled at any time of year.

PAYMENT: To be paid or not to be paid? This is an important question to consider when you approach libraries about offering a special program. No library has an unlimited program budget, so you may need to make some compromises. Perhaps you can bring your own supplies, or do the program for a reduced fee. If a library is interested in hosting your program, but the funds just aren't there, offer to write or cowrite a small grant application that will offset the program cost—and do the legwork of finding an appropriate granting organization.

HELP THE LIBRARY PREPARE: Bryony advises that artists make sure to provide a good outline of the program well in advance, so that the library knows how to market the event. Good things to go over with the library ahead of time include: supplies needed (and who will provide them); room setup (and who is responsible for arranging the room); and any technical equipment needed (and who will arrange setup).

TAPPING INTO GREATER PROGRAM INFRASTRUCTURES

The development of national arts programs that individual states, cities, and towns can tap in to is one significant way that the web has benefited the arts community. A couple of examples include National Novel Writing Month (or NaNoWriMo), National Poetry Month, the Big Read/Dance/ Draw, and National Craft Month.

Major arts organizations administer these programs on a national level by providing marketing toolkits, program how-tos, forums for asking questions of other organizers, and logistics and planning tips. These programs are a great opportunity for practicing artists to raise awareness of their craft and engagement with their community.

Elory Rozner is a Chicago-based consultant whose education innovation consulting firm, Uncommon Classrooms, works with institutions to develop creative educational programs. Through Uncommon Classrooms, Elory administered the Big Draw Chicago, a community engagement initiative (based on a UK program called the Campaign for Drawing) that brings Chicagoans together to draw, think, and share. The program's inaugural schedule in 2012 brought thirty different drawing events to a variety of Chicago locations, including both the Chicago Public Library (CPL) and the Newberry Library.

Like program designers we mentioned earlier in the chapter, Elory approached staff members from CPL and the

Newberry about hosting Big Draw events that related to library activities already underway. The event at CPL ended up focusing on the city's common reading title (*The Book Thief,* by Markus Zusak), while the Newberry Library's drawing event centered on the 150th anniversary of the library's founding. Remember our opening essay, where we mentioned the potential for libraries to serve as "creative crucibles" in the NEA's Creative Placemaking initiative? Well, there's no better example of that than when libraries are included as satellite locations for citywide programs.

Tips for Incorporating Libraries into Large Community Programs

HAVE A PLAN: Figure out the level of planning and involvement you're going to ask of your library (the same goes for other community partners too). Will you invite a library staff member to be on the planning committee? Is each partner responsible for coming up with an event or workshop that fits within the greater program's guidelines? Who will be in charge of making sure each partner has supplies? How will publicity work? Each of these questions (and more) will need to be discussed and planned in advance when approaching your library and other potential partners.

BE FLEXIBLE: Have sample program ideas and guidelines ready, but be open to different approaches. Your library contact will appreciate having some options, but will know what works best in the library and which options are most closely aligned with the library's mission.

INVITE THEM IN: What if your community program doesn't really suit the "satellite" approach? Many libraries have a staff member who is responsible for outreach, which includes literacy activities that take place outside of the library. Even if your large-scale program location is outside or taking place in one location in your town, you can still invite the library to take part (think story times in a park, a craft table at a community center, or a book display at your performing arts center).

Using the Library to Build Your Arts Organization or Business

"I NCUBATION" IN LIBRARIES DOESN'T ONLY MEAN creative or artistic inspiration; libraries also help incubate strategic and organizational skills for arts organizations (including nonprofit groups), and even artists looking to sell their artwork or be compensated for the workshops and classes they offer.

Obviously a library doesn't provide the breadth of resources that, say, a formal arts or business incubator does. Arts and business incubators usually provide some or all of the following:

- Office or studio space
- Office or studio supplies
- Administrative support
- Grants
- Workshops

Libraries of course may offer some of these, but in a more limited way. In this chapter, we hope to shed light on the ways libraries can help organizations and businesses grow, especially in small communities where arts and business incubators don't exist.

NOTE: We focus on library resources like the library's collection of materials and programs and workshops in this chapter, but we don't want to neglect the library's most valuable resource: the people. Should you have questions, or if you're in need of direction when it comes to using these library resources, make sure to ask a staff member for more information. They can help you navigate databases and the library catalog, plus, librarians are great when it comes to "human resources"—knowing the people and groups in the community that may be of help to you.

Resources in the Collection

MANY PUBLIC LIBRARIES—AND CERTAINLY, LIBRARY SYStems—have a healthy collection of materials geared toward small business owners, the self-employed (as many artists are), and nonprofit organizers. Some resources to look for:

- Library brochures or link lists geared to small business owners—these may be physical printouts or link lists on the library's website.

- Check out the library's collection for guides on small business management, on advertising and public relations, and on operating a nonprofit organization.

At the risk of sounding like a broken record, we'll put a plug in for asking a library staff member if you're having trouble finding useful materials on your own. Do research with plenty of time to spare—even if materials are lacking (or are all checked out) when you visit, chances are good that you'll be able to request books from other libraries nearby and have them delivered to your "home" library. Don't be afraid to call or e-mail your library ahead of time to ask the staff to pull some books for you to look at when you come in.

Programs to Look For

We've talked quite a bit about library programs that are focused on art-making, but many libraries also facilitate or host workshops that develop skills for the art professional—someone working to make a living from their art.

Here are several programs and workshops that we know libraries have offered:

- Workshops on using social media to communicate your business's or group's message, using platforms like Twitter, Facebook, Pinterest, and Tumblr. Some workshops get even more specific, with topics like "Social Media Marketing for Small Businesses."

- Make-a-website or start-a-blog workshops

- "The Business of Art" (Minnesota's Hennepin County Library has hosted these)

- Workshops on navigating the grant research and application process

- Marketing and public relations workshops for small businesses

- Workshops on setting up an online shop (We've seen some workshops on specific e-commerce resources, such as Etsy.)

- Self-publishing workshops for authors

- Workshops on how to write query letters to literary agents

- Audition workshops: how to audition well, and where to find good audition material.

Not all libraries have the resources to offer every one of these workshops. But if you and other artists in your community are interested in attending a free workshop on one of the above topics, we recommend talking to your library staff. Librarians who plan programs for their community are always looking for ideas, suggestions, and requests from their community. All the better if you can also recommend a person to facilitate the workshop.

Marketing and Promoting

The public or college library in your community can be an effective way to reach out to a variety of community members. Art businesses or organizations may consider using the library as a venue for promoting the following:

- Calls for artists or craftspeople
- Audition notices
- Events, performances, festivals, and fairs
- Workshops and classes
- Ticket sales

Most libraries have a central bulletin board for posting community events listings and announcements. Check with a staff member to learn about the library's posting policy.

Consider cohosting an event or program with your local library. This is a great way to engage with your community and help them get to know you (and by extension, your group or business). Keep the program topic-oriented to avoid getting too "advertisey," and be aware that many libraries have policies limiting distribution of materials advertising businesses or services.

Here are some examples of programs that an organization or business might cohost with the library:

> *MOST LIBRARIES HAVE A CENTRAL BULLETIN BOARD FOR POSTING COMMUNITY EVENTS LISTINGS AND ANNOUNCEMENTS. CHECK WITH A STAFF MEMBER TO LEARN ABOUT THE LIBRARY'S POSTING POLICY.*

- A free preview night for a community theater, where community members are invited to see actors perform part of a full-length production. This would also work for a local symphony, jazz orchestra, community choir, and other performers.

- Many artist co-ops partner with libraries to keep new art on the library walls (similar to the FDL Visual Arts/Fond du Lac Public Library partnership mentioned in Chapter 6).

- Professional artists and arts educators may consider offering a special free workshop, demonstration, or art class at their public library. Workshops (as we mentioned in Chapter 4) are a great way for people to test-drive a new technique without feeling pressured to commit to a set of formal art classes. Think of a free workshop as a way to develop an engaged group of students, many of whom may turn into paying customers.

Where to Go for More

Public libraries are a great starting point for many business owners or organization leaders, but unless they offer an extensive set of workshops geared toward business and nonprofit organizers, the library's usefulness may plateau.

Academic libraries, on the other hand, often provide more in-depth services that may be available to community businesses or organizations as part of the library's outreach work. If you have a college or university nearby, check the library's website to see what resources are open to community members. Depending on the size (and budget) of the institution, academic libraries may have access to:

- Information about grants and funding for nonprofit organizations or new/small businesses. Librarians will most likely not be able to help you find specific grants, but can guide you through the process of researching and searching for grants and funding opportunities.

- Market research and other business-oriented reports

We highly recommend making an appointment with a reference librarian ahead of time, so you have plenty of time to ask questions and practice with the library's resources. When you're setting up the appointment, let the librarian know what topic you're most interested in learning about. He/she will then be able to tell you if the library has access to that information.

Edinburgh
Waverley

ROYAL MILE

Scotland

United
Kingdom

JOHN
KNOX
HOUSE

HANOVER
STREET

FARMERS
MARKET

Haymarket

Edinburgh

T·K·maxx

The Elephant House

OINK

Alnwick
Castle

ZOO

Arther's Seat   Tattoo

ZOO

Prince street   HARVEY NICHOLS

Loch Ness

NATIONAL
MUSEUM
OF SCOTLAND

Edinburgh

Aberdeen

GALTON Hill

Leith

Preston Field

LOUDONS
CAFE & BAKERY

TOPSHOP

ROYAL MILE

The Meadows

Mimi's   United Kingdom

EH3
9DG   Sainsbury's

fringe

Loch Ness

High Street

OINK

FRINGE

Park   Aberdeen

Edinburgh

Tattoo

United
Kingdom

Alnwick
Castle

Victoria Street

HARVEY NICHOLS

Prince street

FRINGE

Play House

Patisserie

Vintage   Park

mont Blanc

ADDITIONAL LIBRARY-BASED CREATIVITY EXERCISES

In the early part of this book we included exercises inspired by each of our example artists and the ways they use libraries to develop their creative projects. Here we've pulled together an additional set of exercises, tips, and ideas—all of which are right at home in a library setting.

CHECK OUT FIVE NEW ART AND DESIGN BOOKS YOU HAVEN'T EXPLORED YET. Don't limit yourself to what's on the library shelf—check out your library's catalog and order at least two titles from a nonlocal library. No time to dig into them cover to cover? Turn to page 45 in each book and start from there.

CHOOSE AN ILLUSTRATED BOOK BY AN ARTIST YOU ADMIRE. Arm yourself with tools that are different from those used in the original illustrations (if illustrations were done in watercolors, for example, use a flair pen). Spend time practicing making a visual in the style of the chosen artist. Trace an image or two if you want. In the style of the artist, free draw: yourself, a firefighter, a boxer, a princess, and a teacher.*

MAKE LISTS. If you don't know where to begin, here are some ideas to get you started (try walking through the juvenile fiction area, the music section, et cetera, if you need a starting point):

- Favorite books from your childhood

- Favorite artists or songs from middle or high school

- Favorite illustrators

- Places and locations from your favorite childhood books

- Walk along a shelf in the fiction genre area (western, mystery, science fiction). Write down ten of the titles that are most interesting to you.

CARRY A NOTEBOOK EVERYWHERE. Use it when you have an extra fifteen minutes in your library. Make lists (see above), try your hand at drawing the spines lined up on a random bookshelf, write down books to read later or books you've already read or books you never want to read.

LISTEN TO NEW MUSIC. Browse your library's CD section, or investigate Freegal Music (a free music digital library to which many public libraries subscribe). Ask your library staff if they have a local music collection.

GO SOMEWHERE NEW. Live in a city with multiple library branches? Try one in a neighborhood you rarely go to. In town for a few days? Set aside an hour and make the library a stop on your way to other tourist attractions. If your usual library is large enough to have multiple floors, find a new spot to write, read, or work.

OPEN RANDOM BOOKS. Check with a library staff member to see if there is a Dewey decimal system or Library of Congress subject heading chart. Head to a subject you know nothing or relatively little about, and pick out the shiniest book—and the least shiny book—you can find on the subject. Read the first chapter of each.

PICK A COLOR. Take fifteen minutes to go around the library (all different sections) and pick out five books, paying attention only to the color of the book cover, not the title or author. Read the first chapter of each.

USE AN IMAGE TO INSPIRE A FREE-WRITING EXERCISE. Find one in a photography book at the library, or browse for a digitized image in a free database; we've pulled together a selection of them in the Resources list.

DIG INTO AN UNUSUAL DICTIONARY. Some dictionary types and topics include:

- Dream symbols
- Bestiary
- Color dictionary/color theory book
- Tarot
- Runes
- Botanical compendiums

- Astronomy symbols
- Field guides to birds, trees, and plants
- Rocks and minerals

SAVE YOUR LIBRARY RECEIPTS FOR A MONTH. Glue them into your notebook (remember, that one you're carrying around with you?) by date. Wait a week, then look back at all the titles you checked out during that time period. What do you notice about the books or media you checked out? Do you see any themes emerging? Try doodling very simple sketches that depict one, two, or three of those themes.

TAKE NOTES/MAKE LISTS AS YOU READ. Are there words in the book you don't know? Words you love or hate? Try making "visual notes"—instead of jotting down phrases or points to remember later, try sketching these ideas with a pencil or pen instead. Wait a day or two, then look back at these notes. Can you understand the concepts based on the drawings? What about after a week? A month?

TRACE AN ILLUSTRATION FROM A BOOK. Try:

- Botanical books
- Audubon and animal guides
- Children's books
- Cookbooks and food encyclopedias
- Gardening books

In addition to tracing directly, try freehand copying an illustration directly from a book. What do you notice about these two methods of drawing? Which do you like better?

SIT NEXT TO A WINDOW AT YOUR LIBRARY. Use pencil, pen, or paint to make a quick sketch of your view from this window.

WORK WITH A THEME. Choose a section of the library (music, art, photography, gardening, cooking) and create a notebook page of visuals and passages on that theme. Try tracing diagrams, jotting down quotes, and freehand copying some visuals from the books you find. Fill up your notebook page.

BORROW AN IDEA FROM THE SIX-WORD MEMOIR PROJECT. A famous example of a six-word memoir is by Hemingway: "For Sale: baby shoes, never worn." Make a six-word memoir about reading.

CREATE A MURDER MYSTERY INVOLVING YOU IN THE LIBRARY. Where was the body found? Who are the characters in this story? Why are they here? Why are you here? Sketch out a floor plan detailing who's where, and why. Grab a mystery paperback or a classic detective story by Dashiell Hammett or Arthur Conan Doyle to get you in the mood.

*Inspired by Ivan Brunetti's book *Cartooning: Philosophy and Practice.*

Resources

DOWNLOADABLE MATERIALS

Attention librarians: we're happy to provide a selection of free, downloadable materials that you can use in conjunction with this book:

1 Programs to help users get creative in the library
2 Programs and ideas to help users doing creative project research
3 Programs and ideas to encourage "making" in the library
4 Ways to make your library available as an arts venue
5 Tips on creating successful programming partnerships with artists and arts organizations
6 Programs and ideas to help artists promote their work and business

To download these materials, please visit coffeehousepress.org or libraryasincubatorproject.org.

Other Resources

Copyright

- American Society of Composers, Authors and Publishers: http://www.ascap.com
- Copyright Digital Slider, American Library Association: http://librarycopyright.net/resources/digitalslider/
- Creative Commons: http://creativecommons.org
- Stanford Copyright and Fair Use Center: http://fairuse.stanford.edu
- u.s. Copyright Office: http://www.copyright.gov

Libraries and Library Advocacy

- American Library Association, Office of Library Advocacy: http://www.ala.org/offices/ola
- Authors for Libraries: http://authorsforlibraries.org
- BoingBoing: http://boingboing.net
- EveryLibrary, the Political Action Committee for Libraries: http://everylibrary.org
- Institute for Museum and Library Services: http://www.imls.gov
- Online Computer Library Center (OCLC): http://oclc.org
- Save Libraries: http://savelibraries.org
- WorldCat: http://www.worldcat.org

Creative Communities

- [ALOUD], Los Angeles Public Library Foundation: http://www.lfla.org/aloud/

- American Craft Council: http://www.craftcouncil.org
- The Big Read, National Endowment for the Arts: http://www.neabigread.org
- BONK! Performance Series: http://bonkperformanceseries.wordpress.com
- Books and Adventures: http://matthewfinch.me
- The Campaign for Drawing: http://www.campaignfordrawing.org
- Center for Book Arts, New York City: http://www.centerforbookarts.org/
- Creative Placemaking, National Endowment for the Arts: http://arts.gov/sites/default/files/CreativePlacemaking-Paper.pdf
- Handmade Librarian: http://www.handmadelibrarian.com
- Hands Occupied: http://www.handsoccupied.com
- The Idea Box, Oak Park Public Library: http://oppl.org/event-type/idea-box
- I Street Press, Sacramento Public Library: http://www.saclibrary.org/istreet/
- Lifetime Arts: http://www.lifetimearts.org/
- Line Assembly: http://lineassembly.com
- Make It @ Your Library: http://makeitatyourlibrary.org
- *MAKE* magazine: http://makezine.com/
- National Novel Writing Month: http://www.nanowrimo.org
- Poem in Your Pocket Day: http://www.poets.org/page.php/prmID/406
- Rainbow Rumpus: http://www.rainbowrumpus.org

Online Digital Collections and Galleries

- 50 Watts
- AIGA Design Archive
- ArchiveGrid
- Art, Music, and Recreation Center at the San Francisco Public Library
- Biodiversity Heritage Library
- Boston Athenaeum
- Bridgeman Art Library Digital Collections
- Brooklyn Visual Heritage
- Central Inspiration at the Edinburgh Central Library
- Getty Research Institute Digital Collections
- The Hatchery at the Glasgow School of Art Library
- International Music Scores Library Project
- Iowa Digital Library
- Library of Congress Digital Collections
- The Morgan Library & Museum
- Museum of Performance & Design
- New York Public Library Digital Gallery
- Public Art Archive
- Rare Book School Exhibitions
- The Sketchbook Project at the Brooklyn Art Library
- Smithsonian Galaxy of Images
- Special Collections of the University of St Andrews
- University of Wisconsin–Madison Digital Collections
- Wellcome Images
- The Wolfsonian–Florida International University

ONLINE MULTIMEDIA RESOURCES AND COLLECTIONS

- Alan Lomax Music Archive
- Ballroom Dance Archives
- Black Dance Archives Project
- British Film Institute National Archive
- Dance Heritage Coalition
- Digital Dance Archives
- Free Music Archive
- National Jukebox
- Scottish Dance Archives
- Smithsonian Folkways
- The Wilson Library: Southern Folklife Collection–University of North Carolina

DEWEY DECIMAL NUMBERS

- Full list may be found here:
  http://www.library.illinois.edu/ugl/about/dewey.html

FIGURE LIST

- PAGE 10: Wendy MacNaughton, from *The San Francisco Public Library in Its Own Words.* Illustration. Originally published on the *Rumpus* (therumpus.net) in 2011. Reprinted by permission of the artist.

- PAGE 14: Sigrid Schmeisser, *140 Characters.* Animation. 2013. Part of the Interactive Art Trail at Edinburgh Central Library, Edinburgh, Scotland. Reprinted by permission of the artist.

- PAGE 17: Wendy MacNaughton, from *The San Francisco Public Library in Its Own Words.* Illustration. Originally published on the *Rumpus* (therumpus.net) in 2011. Reprinted by permission of the artist.

- PAGE 19: Mark Reigelman, *The Reading Nest.* Installation. 2013. Reprinted by permission of the artist.

- PAGE 28: Pushpi Bagchi, *Youth.* Installation. 2013. Part of the Interactive Art Trail at Edinburgh Central Library, Edinburgh, Scotland. Reprinted by permission of the artist.

- PAGE 35: Jamie Powell Sheppard, *Jefferson Market Tower.* Photograph. 2012. Reprinted by permission of the artist.

- PAGE 36: Jamie Powell Sheppard, *STW Window and Stacks.* Photograph. 2012. Reprinted by permission of the artist.

- PAGE 40: Doreen Kennedy, *Book Grid Series 1–6.* Photograph collage. 2011. Reprinted by permission of the artist.

- PAGE 46–47: Chris Gaul, *Library Tuner.* Installation. 2012. Reprinted by permission of the artist.

- PAGE 48–49: Chris Gaul, *Library Spectrogram.* Spectrogram wall chart. 2012. Reprinted by permission of the artist.
- PAGE 54: Joseph Mills, "If Librarians Were Honest." First published in *Sending Christmas Cards to Huck and Hamlet,* Press 53, 2012. Reprinted by permission of the artist.
- PAGE 56: Laura Damon-Moore, *Herb Investigation.* Traced from *Home Gardener's Cookbook* by Marjorie P. Blanchard (Charlotte, VT: Garden Way Publishing Co., 1974). Reprinted by permission of the artist.
- PAGE 63–65: Carol Chase Bjerke, *Point of Departure.* Artist's book. 1986. Reprinted by permission of the artist.
- PAGE 66: Carol Chase Bjerke, *The Pocket Mountain Meditator.* Artist's book. 1994. Reprinted by permission of the artist.
- PAGE 69: Stephen Crowe, *our cubehouse still rocks.* Based on *Finnegans Wake* by James Joyce (page 5). Digital illustration. 2010. Reprinted by permission of the artist.
- PAGE 71: Stephen Crowe, *her grace o' malice.* Based on *Finnegans Wake* by James Joyce (page 22). Digital illustration. 2010. Reprinted by permission of the artist.
- PAGE 73: Dan Augustine, *Everything is Fragile.* Illustration. 2012. Reprinted by permission of the artist.
- PAGE 75: Kathleen Behrens, *Untitled.* Hand-drawn map. 2013. Reprinted by permission of the artist.
- PAGE 79: Brian P. Hall, "Study Bible: The Parable of Natural Law" (excerpt). Reprinted by permission of the artist.
- PAGE 82: Laura Damon-Moore, *Flower Investigation.* Based on photographs in *The Complete Guide to Garden Flowers: An*

Encyclopedia of Garden Planning by Herbert Askwith (New York: Barnes, 1961). Reprinted by permission of the artist.

- PAGE 91: Nicola Dickson, *Joseph Banks* and *Daniel Solander* from the *Wedgwood Blue* series. Pencil and gouache. 2011. Reprinted by permission of the artist.

- PAGE 96: Kristen Baumlier, *Vegetare Print No. 1.* 2011. Reprinted by permission of the artist.

- PAGE 97: Kristen Baumlier, *Crude Oil/Carboniferous Forest Print No. 1.* 2011. Reprinted by permission of the artist.

- PAGE 103: Kristin Hammargren in *Discovering Austen.* Photograph by Grant Griffiths. 2012. Reprinted by permission of the artist.

- PAGE 107: Rita Mae Reese, "Apocrypha: Flannery and the Book of Tobit." Reprinted by permission of the artist.

- PAGE 109: Laura Damon-Moore, *Rose Investigation.* Traced from *The Rockwells' Complete Book of Roses: A Practical Guide to the Uses, Selection, Planting, Care, Exhibition, and Propagation of Roses of All Types* by F. F. Rockwell and Esther C. Grayson (Garden City, NY: Doubleday, 1958). Reprinted by permission of the artist.

- PAGE 111: Spinner's End at Princeton Public Library. Photograph by SKY. 2012. Reprinted by permission of the artist.

- PAGE 115: Cheryl Sorg, *Booklover Thumbprint.* Mixed media. Reprinted by permission of the artist.

- PAGE 120: Lisa Cinar, coloring card from Draw Me a Lion set. 2012. Reprinted by permission of the artist.

- PAGE 121: Lisa Cinar, flower kids print from Draw Me a Lion set. 2012. Reprinted by permission of the artist.
- PAGE 143: Dr. Michael Salcman, "The Dog Speaks." First published in the *Hopkins Review*, Vol. 3 No. 2 (New Series), Spring 2010, page 210. Also appears in *The Enemy of Good Is Better* (Washington, DC: Orchises Press, 2011). Reprinted by permission of the artist.
- PAGE 144: Dr. Michael Salcman, "Cutting Apples." First published in *Alaska Quarterly Review*, Vol. 27 (No. 1 and 2), Spring and Summer 2010, page 223. Reprinted on *Poetry Daily*, June 21, 2010. Also appears in *The Enemy of Good Is Better* (Washington, DC: Orchises Press, 2011). Reprinted by permission of the artist.
- PAGE 149: Trent Miller, *THEY Offered US Fish.* Charcoal on paper. 2012. Reprinted by permission of the artist.
- PAGE 151: Seth Jambor and Alissa Razzano in *Eurydice,* in the Page to Stage Series at the Princeton Public Library. Photograph by the Princeton Public Library. 2011. Reprinted by permission.
- PAGE 153: Cast of *Einstein's Dreams* rehearsing for the Page to Stage series at Princeton Public Library. Photograph by Ally Blumenfeld. 2012. Reprinted by permission of the artist.
- PAGE 167: Melissa Kolstad, *The Detritus Project.* Mixed media/collage. 2012. Reprinted by permission of the artist.
- PAGE 172–173: Children's programming by PlayBods. Photographs by Kim Glassby and Bryony Pritchard. 2012. Reprinted by permission of the artist.

- PAGE 178: The Big Draw—Chicago logo. Provided by Elory Rozner. Reprinted by permission of the artist.
- PAGE 180: Lisa Occhipinti, *Bookmobile Duo.* Altered books. Reprinted by permission of the artist.
- PAGE 192–193: Chu Chia Chi, *Capturing Scotland & Edinburgh in Watercolours.* Watercolor. 2013. Part of the Interactive Art Trail at Edinburgh Central Library, Edinburgh, Scotland. Reprinted by permission of the artist.

CREDITS

ARTISTS, WRITERS, AND PERFORMERS

Below are biographies and additional information about each of the artists, writers, and performers who are highlighted in this book. Special thanks to each of them for sharing their work and experiences with us.

DAN AUGUSTINE is an illustrator and designer from Shorewood, Wisconsin. He is associate creative director and partner at Noise Inc., a Milwaukee ad agency, and teaches courses at Marquette University and the University of Wisconsin–Milwaukee.

PUSHPI BAGCHI is a communications designer currently based in Edinburgh, Scotland.

KRISTEN BAUMLIÉR's work spans the full spectrum of interdisciplinary media, including performance, installation, video, and audio. In 2005, Baumliér began performing as the "Petroleum Pop Princess," a pop icon engaging viewers about oil consumerism. She has performed at the Mattress Factory, the Cleveland Center for Contemporary Art, and the Headlands Center for the Arts. Her work has shown at the Sculpture Center in Cleveland, Ohio; Hotcakes Gallery in Milwaukee, Wisconsin; and the UNI Gallery of Art. Her videos have screened in New Zealand, Serbia, England, and the United States.

CAROL CHASE BJERKE is a photographer, book artist, and multimedia artist from Wisconsin. She is a visual arts educator who has taught at universities, colleges, and special programs around the Midwest.

CHU CHIA CHI is a visual artist and illustrator from Taiwan. She recently completed her degree from Edinburgh College of Art.

LISA CINAR is the creator of the online shop Draw Me a Lion, which specializes in imaginative prints, cards, and activities for kids of all ages. She is also the author and illustrator of two picture books, *The Day It all Blew Away* and *Paulina P. (for Petersen)*, both published by Simply Read Books. She currently teaches three classes on illustration for picture books in the Continuing Studies Department at the Emily Carr Institute of Art & Design, and writes a blog on picture book illustration called *IHeartPicturebooks*.

STEPHEN CROWE is a graphic designer and illustrator who lives in Paris, France. His blog about drawing moments from *Finnegans Wake* is called *Wake in Progress*.

NICOLA DICKSON is a painter and multimedia artist from Australia. Since childhood, plants, animals, and the natural world have fascinated her. This interest led her to two bachelor's degrees, first in veterinary science and later in visual arts. Nicola completed a PhD in 2010 that examined perceptions of the exotic in Australia. Her work shows around Australia in solo and group exhibitions.

CHRIS GAUL explores the potential for art and design to create moments of mindfulness and discovery in everyday life. He studied visual communication design and international studies at Australia's University of Technology–Sydney (UTS), works as an artist and visual designer, and teaches in the UTS School of Design. His work has been exhibited at the Art Gallery of New South Wales, the Brooklyn Museum in New York, and work from his recent project *The Art of Everyday Things* was exhibited as part of Sydney Design 2011. In 2012, Chris was the artist-in-residence at the UTS libraries.

BRIAN P. HALL is a writer and educator whose fiction and essays have appeared in the *Palo Alto Review, Lullwater Review,* the *G.W. Review, Exquisite Corpse, Shadowbox,* and the *Chronicle of Higher Education,* among others. Brian teaches English at Cuyahoga Community College in Cleveland, Ohio.

KRISTIN HAMMARGREN received her master of fine arts degree from the University of Wisconsin–Madison School of Theater and Drama in 2012. She works in Wisconsin as an actor and theater educator.

DOREEN KENNEDY is an Irish artist working with photography and graphic design. Recent exhibitions include shows in New York City and Dublin, Galway, and Kilkenny in Ireland.

MELISSA KOLSTAD is a collagist and ephemeralist who lives and works in Fond du Lac, Wisconsin. She is an active member of the Fond du Lac Visual Arts collective, an organization that works closely with the Fond du Lac Public Library. She is also a member of the Fond du Lac Public Library's board.

WENDY MACNAUGHTON is an illustrator and graphic journalist in San Francisco. Her art has appeared in the *New York Times*, NPR, *Juxtapoz, GOOD, Time Out New York, 7x7,* and *Gizmodo.* She has created magazine cover images for *7x7* and *Edible San Francisco.*

TRENT MILLER is a visual artist, art educator, and library program coordinator for the Madison Public Library in Madison, Wisconsin. He coordinates the Bubbler, Madison Public Library's maker program.

JOSEPH MILLS is an educator and poet. He is on the faculty at the University of North Carolina School of the Arts. His most recent book of poetry, *Sending Christmas Cards to Huck and Hamlet,* was published by Press 53 in March 2012.

BRANDON MONOKIAN is a theater artist in the New York City/New Jersey area. His recent projects include *Grimm Women,* which he wrote and directed, and *The Vagina Monologues,* which he directed. Brandon's other directing credits include Revolutionary Readings and the Page to Stage series for the Princeton Public Library. Brandon also works as a professional actor in New York City and New Jersey, and writes for multiple online magazines.

LISA OCCHIPINTI is an artist, photographer, author and instructor based in Venice, California. She has written and illustrated *The Repurposed Library* (STC/Abrams) and her Bookmobiles have been included in a compendium on paper arts titled *Papercraft* (Gestalten). Most recently she has contributed as an essayist to *The Laws of Subtraction* by Matthew May (McGraw-Hill).

BRYONY PRITCHARD AND KIM GLASSBY are visual and performance artists based in Leeds, England. Together they form a group called Playbods, which brings storytelling and art-making experiences for young children and their families to UK libraries.

RITA MAE REESE is the author of *The Alphabet Conspiracy*, and has received a Rona Jaffe Foundation Writers' Award, a Stegner fellowship, and a Discovery/The Nation award. Her work has been nominated for a Pushcart Prize and has appeared in numerous journals and anthologies. She lives in Madison, Wisconsin.

ELORY ROZNER is the founder and principal of Uncommon Classrooms. She is also the coordinator for the Big Draw–Chicago.

DR. MICHAEL SALCMAN is a former chairman of the Department of Neurosurgery at the University of Maryland and a former president of Baltimore's Contemporary Museum. He is currently president of the CityLit Project in Baltimore, and is a special lecturer for Osher Institute, Towson University. His poems have appeared in the *Ontario Review*, *Harvard Review*, *Raritan*, and in many other publications. His newest collection, *The Enemy of Good is Better*, was published in January 2011 by Orchises Press. Three poems by Dr. Salcman have been nominated for a Pushcart Prize.

SIGRID SCHMEISSER is a graphic designer from Austria, currently based in Edinburgh, Scotland.

JAMIE POWELL SHEPPARD, a Dallas native, is a fine art black-and-white film photographer currently living in Louisville, Kentucky. Light and shadow, abstract composition, and texture are what drive her need to photograph a particular subject. She especially tends to be drawn to everyday scenes that she feels are overlooked. Jamie develops her own film and occasionally has been guilty of falling asleep while clutching her latest adopted vintage camera.

CHERYL SORG is a multimedia artist based in Boston, Massachusetts. Her work has been exhibited in solo and group exhibitions in galleries and museums across the United States, including WorkSpace in New York City; the Copley Society of Art, the Photographic Resource Center, and the Forest Hills Trust in Boston; the Eric Phleger Gallery, the San

Diego Art Institute, and the Museum of Photographic Arts in San Diego; the Long Beach Museum of Art; and the Torrance Art Museum. Her work is included in the esteemed Allan Chasanoff Bookworks Collection in New York City, and is referenced in the book *A Companion to Herman Melville*, edited by Wyn Kelley, in the chapter entitled "Creating Icons: Melville in Visual Media and Popular Culture," written by Elizabeth Schultz, as well as a book entitled *Four-Word Self-Help*, by Patti Digh.

CHRISTI WEINDORF completed the master of library and information science program at San Jose State University in 2012 and now works as a librarian. Over the past two years, she has worked and interned with the Museum of Performance and Design, the Dance Heritage Coalition, the King Library at San Jose State University, and the Stanford University libraries. Before pursuing an MLIS, Christi worked in arts education and earned a master's from Trinity Laban Conservatoire of Music and Dance.

SOURCES FOR CREATIVITY EXERCISES

The creativity exercises in this book came to be through a number of different processes. Some of them we conceived on our own, or they are the written-down version of exercises we do in our own art-making and writing. Others are traditional or commonly used creativity exercises that we've adapted for library spaces or collections. Some are borrowed from awesome art educators and artists, and we've added library flavor. Still others were contributed by the writers, artists, and performers we interviewed for this book. Those contributions are noted next to the relevant exercises.

Contact Information

Please visit us online at libraryasincubatorproject.org
and booktoartclub.org.

Follow us on Facebook, Twitter, Pinterest, and Tumblr.
E-mail us at libraryasincubatorproject@gmail.com.

COFFEE HOUSE PRESS

The mission of Coffee House Press is to publish exciting, vital, and enduring authors of our time; to delight and inspire readers; to contribute to the cultural life of our community; and to enrich our literary heritage. By building on the best traditions of publishing and the book arts, we produce books that celebrate imagination, innovation in the craft of writing, and the many authentic voices of the American experience.

Visit us at coffeehousepress.org.

Books in Action is an initiative by Coffee House Press to publish works and develop programs that encourage and nurture literary arts beyond the page, highlighting people and organizations working to further interdisciplinary collaborations, reader engagement, and nontraditional means of accessing the reading experience.

For more information about Books in Action titles and programs, visit coffeehousepress.org/books-in-action.

LITERATURE
is not the same thing as
PUBLISHING

COFFEE HOUSE PRESS IN THE STACKS

Inspired by the Library as Incubator Project, the Writers and Readers Library Residency Program places readers and writers in residence at public, school, and specialty libraries to create a body of work that will inspire a broader public to engage with their local libraries in new and meaningful ways, and to encourage artists and the general public to think about libraries as creative spaces.

LITTLE FREE LIBRARY

In an ongoing partnership with Little Free Library, Coffee House Press has, since 2011, donated more than six thousand books to the libraries. Coffee House Press titles have traveled with Little Free Libraries from the first few prototypes in Wisconsin and Minnesota to installations in forty-two countries worldwide. Coffee House Press is also collaborating with them on *My Little Free Library* by Margret Aldrich, to be published in Fall 2015.

FUNDER ACKNOWLEDGMENTS

COFFEE HOUSE PRESS is an independent, nonprofit literary publisher. Our books are made possible through the generous support of grants and gifts from many foundations, corporate giving programs, state and federal support, and through donations from individuals who believe in the transformational power of literature. Coffee House Press receives major operating support from Amazon, the Bush Foundation, the Jerome Foundation, the McKnight Foundation, from the National Endowment for the Arts—a federal agency, from Target, and in part from a grant provided by the Minnesota State Arts Board through an appropriation by the Minnesota State Legislature from the State's general fund and its arts and cultural heritage fund with money from the vote of the people of Minnesota on November 4, 2008, and a grant from the Wells Fargo Foundation of Minnesota. Coffee House Press also receives support from: several anonymous donors; Rand Alexander; Suzanne Allen; Elmer L. and Eleanor J. Andersen Foundation; Mary & David Anderson Family Foundation; Around Town Agency; Patricia Beithon; Bill Berkson; the E. Thomas Binger and Rebecca Rand Fund of the Minneapolis Foundation; the Patrick and Aimee Butler Family Foundation; the Buuck Family Foundation; Claire Casey; Jane Dalrymple-Hollo; Ruth Dayton; Dorsey

& Whitney, LLP; Mary Ebert and Paul Stembler; Chris Fischbach and Katie Dublinski; Fredrikson & Byron, P.A.; Katharine Freeman; Sally French; Jeffrey Hom; Carl and Heidi Horsch; Kenneth Kahn; Alex and Ada Katz; Stephen and Isabel Keating; the Kenneth Koch Literary Estate; Kathryn and Dean Koutsky; the Lenfestey Family Foundation; Carol and Aaron Mack; George Mack; Leslie Larson Maheras; Gillian McCain; Mary McDermid; Sjur Midness and Briar Andresen; the Nash Foundation; Peter & Jennifer Nelson; the Rehael Fund of the Minneapolis Foundation; Schwegman, Lundberg & Woessner, P.A.; Kiki Smith; Jeffrey Sugerman and Sarah Schultz; Nan Swid; Patricia Tilton; the Archie D. & Bertha H. Walker Foundation; Stu Wilson and Mel Barker; the Woessner Freeman Family Foundation; Margaret and Angus Wurtele; and many other generous individual donors,

To you and our many readers across the country, we send our thanks for your continuing support.

ERINN BATYKEFER is a librarian, a writer, and a lifelong do-it-yourselfer. She's worked in libraries almost constantly since she was fifteen—both as a staffer and as a writer scribbling away at the back of the 811s. She earned an MFA in writing and a master of library and information studies from the University of Wisconsin–Madison. Her first poetry collection, *Allegheny, Monongahela* (Red Hen Press, 2009) won the Benjamin Saltman Poetry Prize.

LAURA DAMON-MOORE is a librarian, blogger, and avid art-maker in her spare time. Laura received her master's degree in library and information studies from the University of Wisconsin–Madison in 2012 and graduated from Beloit College with a double major in literary studies and theatre arts (acting) in 2008. She lives in Madison, Wisconsin with her husband, James, and her chinchilla, Barnaby Jones.